SPIRITUAL COUNSELING IN MEDICINE

✦

Theories and Techniques of Counseling During Stressful Life Events, Serious Illnesses, and Palliative Care

Carlo Lazzari

iUniverse, Inc.
New York   Bloomington

SPIRITUAL COUNSELING IN MEDICINE

Theories and Techniques of Counseling During Stressful Life Events, Serious Illnesses, and Palliative Care

iUniverse books may be ordered through booksellers or by contacting:

iUniverse
1663 Liberty Drive
Bloomington, IN 47403
www.iuniverse.com
1-800-Authors (1-800-288-4677)

ISBN: 978-0-595-53264-3 (pbk)
ISBN: 978-0-595-63319-7 (ebk)

Library of Congress Control Number: 2008940935

Printed in the United States of America

iUniverse rev. date: 03/12/09

This book is dedicated to my sister Silvia whose support and affection has helped me to bring this work to completion.

Contents

Preface

The help to needy people. Our involvement for sustaining the spirit of those who feel down. Our attitude to spend part of our time for assisting people with serious illnesses. Our joy to deliver a word of comfort to whom asks for it. These are all forms of helping relationships. Basically, the desire to make us available to whom we regard as needy, poor, sad, seems that is written in our genetic system. Moreover, by donating ourselves to other human beings we strengthen their identity, self-esteem, and joy to live. At the same time, the awareness that we have been of help to others with our presence, allows us to increase our psychic comfort. But this humanitarian action is collective, and spiritual counseling is a dialogue between two human beings. Thus, spirituality also means growing together in a shared spirit of brotherhood and sisterhood with people who suffer and are ill. This to say that it is really through the actions of support of ill people that we can promote, through their spiritual growth, a better psychological and physical health. At the same time, those who feel sustained and beloved by us are able to join again life, even if facing a limited life expectancy. Other times, underprivileged people, people who suffer, who are victims of abuses and poverty feel having a limited "existential expectancy", that is to say, they feel that they have not enough personal resources to gain access to happiness and satisfaction. Also in this instance, spiritual counseling, by using the same strategies of intervention applied in hospital to very sick persons, can restore a more positive outlook for life, and can increase personal resilience. Nevertheless, spiritual counseling is always a match between counselor's personal inclinations and the acquisition of specific interpersonal strategies. Indeed, both are helpful to offer to needy people an efficient and efficacious relief. Moreover, unlike other counseling strategies, spiritual counseling is a form of helping relationship offering a way of mutual aid and growth: both patient and counselor move towards higher degrees of spiritual complexity. Both feel sustained and beloved, and are able to perfection one's own life, to perceive an unexpected and mutual solidarity, and to take back the strengths to return to live with joy and hope. Therefore, spiritual counseling is a dynamic approach to life, more than a mere technique. It is a dialogue on life and spirit that comprises people: counselors, clients, families, community, doctors, nurses, health workers, helpers, etc. Spiritual counseling is also a search of (other) meanings and is deep and contemplative in its nature. Consequently, any word, gesture, glance of a counselor carries high symbolic and interpersonal values for a patient. Basically, a helping relationship is a moment of mutual support and dialogue. However, really because it deals with so important moments and is natural and spontaneous, that it is important to prepare us with conscience to know the dynamics and the essential passages of it. This will allow us to become professional helpers or, more accurately, people able to help with science and conscience other fellows who need our help. For what concerns my personal experience in religion, spirituality, and health, I shall say that I have practiced as a doctor in hospitals with patients with serious and terminal diseases. During this period, I have noticed the power of spirituality and faith during each stage of an illness, even for those who were not in the latest stages. Thereafter, I continued my experience as a missionary psychologist in developing countries. Here, too, I witnessed the power of faith, religion, and spirituality on personal well-being and resilience of needy people. The same experience I collected when operating as volunteer in social centers for homeless people. In these places, I started to feel how spirituality could be enhanced not only by feelings of brotherhood but also by involvement in the sacred art. The opportunity offered by symbolism and meditation through the aid of sacred paintings, poetries, or hand-made works seemed to offer an extra-advantage for developing spiritual growth.

1
General aspects of spiritual counseling

✦

1.1. FOREWORDS

The search of the spiritual self
is the highest journey
in human history.

Spiritual counseling is presented as a privileged intervention on clients with existential plights, serious illnesses, or terminal diseases. In addition, not solely is this counseling a diagnostic and interpretative approach, but also a unique and special way to live the relationship between helper and client. This encounter is characterized by an intense involvement of a helper in client's experience and existence, and by a helper's respect for client's condition and sufferings. Usually spiritual counseling requires a specific training where a counselor learns topics about the philosophical, existential and spiritual aspects of human life. Because of this renovated point of observation, a counselor shall thus consider a client with a serious/terminal illness as a "living person". This is to say that any patient becomes a person who seeks assistance from a helper during a personal process of attribution of meanings to what is happening. Thus, spiritual counseling can help in this direction. In addition, it is the helper's task to get the required professional training in order to be considered by clients as a valid "companion", and as an "assistant" during the *re*discovery of life.

Essentially, any person involved in the health system will face a daily request for counseling coming from his/her own clients. Although counseling per se requires specific strategies and learning, given enough time and teaching, any person could master basic and advanced strategies of spiritual counseling. In addition, health practice will essentially lead to specific counseling themes that require a total involvement of any health operator with the own clients. This bilateral involvement accentuates psychological, philosophical, existential themes in both participants: helper and client. Consequently, counseling of patients in the health system usually occurs along peculiar pathways, some being standard for all health clients, while others deriving from specific and subjective reaction of each patient to diagnosis, treatment, and hospitalization. Nevertheless, in each stage of care and illness, spiritual counseling will embrace a definite awareness in specific humanistic fields, mainly:

- Psychology and counseling.
- Existential philosophy and spiritual care.
- Occupational and expressive therapy.

In this part, it is suggested that the need for spirituality is somehow an experience that steams out of a person during moments of tribulation, existential conflicts, diseases, and unpredicted stops to daily plans. Usually, crises during diseases can be interpreted as a stop to existential projects, like a marital conflict is a halt to projects of personal development. Besides, as it happens during sudden stops, any patient will try to identify alternative venues to move forwards, especially when the original goals can no longer be achieved: health, family, work, wealth, etc. Therefore, in order to focus on the idea of spirituality as "progression in one's own life", and "spiritual counseling also as an instrument to re-activate movement", we shall try an initial approach to the "philosophy of inner movements", as a template to select some core concepts in spiritual counseling[1].

1.2. SPIRITUAL COUNSELING AND THE EIGHT DIRECTIONS OF INNER MOVEMENTS

If you love your neighbor
you're are on the way
to heal yourself.

Usually, we can spiritually move only in two directions: towards the self or against the self. If the prevailing movement is "towards the self", a man becomes a friend for himself and others. If, instead, "against the self" succeeds, a person becomes a sort of persecutor with projects to abort any movement towards life and "moving", in self and others. Also during spiritual counseling, we meet two people each one involved in the encounter with his/her own existential project. In effect, not only is it important that a client is willing to self-heal, and to progress towards existential healing, but also a counselor should be life-oriented, and people-oriented. Furthermore, spiritual counseling is a tandem movement, and no achievement can be obtained with disjoined spiritual projects. Therefore, a progression in spiritual counseling is enhanced by the development of a dyad, counselor-client. In contrast, a standard unidirectional approach is less effective when embracing only a unilateral growth: only in the client. Consequently, in spiritual counseling, any development is always reciprocal, as it is the benefit. The same applies to growth: client and counselor both grow and develop when being one with the other, and "moving" one towards the other. Thus, "moving forward", or simply "going together", will be considered as the kinetic and visible aspect of spiritual development in the dyad. Actually, by evaluating how a person moves in the world, we are also able to establish what are the events of his soul. As Balzac states: "Any movement has its own definition for its own and it comes from the soul".[2] Accordingly, man's movement in his life represents the imago of his soul, as the synchrony of his progression with other human fellows symbolizes a measure of his civilization. Thus, by constructing a bipolar model along three alignments, we can identify eight directions of spiritual movements, and how they relate to social and personal growth. The poles are four and exactly:

- TS: *Towards the Self.* It means acting and living by aiming to self-care, healing, personal well-being and private progression. However, no particular care is taken for the well-being and progression intended as a social dimension.

- TO: *Towards the Others.* It means acting and living also to promote a social progression and social well-being. This person, moving in this direction, feels that the own existential goal can be reached only by altruistic and philanthropic actions. Nevertheless, the self can be or not at the center of his/her attention.

- AS: *Against the Self.* It means that there is no action and behavior intended for the promotion of a spiritual and psychological growth. Although we can find actions apparently conducted for the self (e.g., an hedonistic behavior), a practical look would disconfirm a positive result towards a better and personal spiritual, physical, and psychological well-being.

- AO: *Against the Others.* It means that this person is acting solely for facilitating the advancement of the self. No social and philanthropic movement can be witnessed. The self is central and exclusive. Growth and progression are intended as personal goals and no interpersonal sharing can be witnessed.

It seems singular to talk about "moving against other people" in a helping profession. But it should be interpreted as a perspective of life or, better, as a spiritual perspective. Basically, "Against the Others" is anything that is not done for the good of others. Furthermore, even a slight sense of personal "protection" of a counselor against a full involvement with difficult clients is somehow separating two movements, the own aspiration and the client's needs. For example, I can cite an episode that came to chronicle in Italy, and that was about a nurse performing unauthorized "merciful killings" of old terminal patients. Here, we find a movement that is "against the others" but confused, by the nurse, as "towards others". In addition, we find an unconscious "towards the self" in order to reduce personal conflicts and stress. Thus, spiritual counseling is a continuous analysis of motivations, directions, and perspectives both in counselors and clients. Practically, it is a back-and-forth appraisal of the real intentions that counselors and clients hold in order to move to secure understandings of life and its meanings. For example, Saint Teresa of Ávila talking about her inner turmoil, and aware that what seems right not always is really right, said: "Sometimes I had the perception that the demons were playing soccer with my soul, unable to escape. You cannot say how much you suffer, the soul seeks help, but the Lord does not allow it to find it; what's left to soul is the free will, but it is not clear. It is like having the eyes bandaged…".[3] As a result, we get the following categories of the spiritual movements during interpersonal relations, depending of the way the Self relates to the others:

1. *Towards the self:* the dimension "Other" has little relevance, and a subject is centered to get his/her own well-being for the spiritual growth of the self. It can happen because s/he feels empty, sick, or simply because with poor spiritual resources to be shared. Here, one's personal growth has the priority. The probe statement can be: "I think that my personal well-being is very relevant for me. However, I do not much bother about how others feels and live".

2. *Towards the self and towards the others*: the personal perception of spiritual movement is not separated from the idea that s/he can have a companion in this travel. Practically, a person perceives the self as alone and meaningless unless s/he is able to share with others the pleasure of spiritual growth, and the gifts of spirituality. The usual remark can be: "I feel that spirituality has an important role in my life. I would also like to share this journey with others".

3. *Towards the others*: it is a condition of total self-neglect. Here, the Self cannot feel separated from the Others. Thus, there is a total identification with the "other from self" to the point that a spiritual movement has a meaning only if made together with others in a spirit of brotherhood. In addition, a philanthropic aspiration is found together with a total dedication to the good of other people. The person who embraces this perspective can even donate his/her own life to save other people's life. A sense of this spiritual dimension can be found in the Prayer for the Peace of Saint Francis who asks to the Lord: "…to love instead of being loved".[4] The familiar comment could be: "I find a profound interest in other people who steams from my spiritual and religious background. I believe that my life would be meaningless if I cannot be of any help to others". According to Viktor Frankl: "The existential fullness and the self-fulfillment in the human being is reached when we become concerned about other human beings and forget our Selves".[5] Thus, in order to be happy and healthy, and psychologically mature, according to Frankl, a person should be able to direct the own existential focus towards the others and interested about the others.[6] Similarly, the idea of Confucius is that "a person is realized only in his integration (his 'co-humanization') with others".[7]

4. *Towards the others and against the self*: it is a false spirituality. For example, a counselor nourishes the false perception that helping is negating the self. In this instance, there is confusion between the boundaries of the Self and the spiritual circle where the client stays. In this dimension, we can find also some examples of sectarian rituals, where a subject harms him/herself to gain full acceptance and love from the peer group. Here, there is no spiritual growth, and the occurrence of religious intolerance is a common finding. A common statement can be: "I believe that I cannot live without the approval of the people I trust. And making sacrifices to please them is a way in which I express my spirituality".

5. *Against the Self.* In this dimension, there is a total stop in the spiritual as well as in the life project and movement. Basically, a person believes that s/he does not deserve to live. Usually, this person is facing parental injunctions (see Transactional Analysis) that go in this direction. In fact, as Transactional Analysis shows, many violated children receive parental injunctions of the kind "Don't be" and "Don't exist". Consequently, during their life, they may unconsciously boycott counselors' attempts to promote their well-being. In addition, spirituality and love are sometimes lived as foreign to their lives because do not they feel deign of attention and love. However, spirituality and religion can still play an important role in moderating parental messages, and in providing them with alternative internal models or life-injunctions ("Be!", "Exist!", "Be yourself!"). Typically, the existence of an unconditional love from heaven entities, the Lord and others, may hamper negative tendencies to abandon spiritual counseling and may reinforce their quest for self-cure and self-actualization.

6. *Against the Self and Against the Others.* Many antisocial personality people may be lead by these two drives. The combination of hindrances in interpersonal relations makes spiritual counseling difficult. However, these people should be kindly moved towards more positive positions in the spiritual star scheme: always moving in the clockwise direction: TS-AO, and finally TS. Initially, these people might not be inclined to altruism, and the direction they would like to make in the self-healing process, is accepted as long as they feel it would be of some personal benefit. Thus, spirituality can be still accepted as a holistic therapy, with differential degrees of mysticism and religion. Nevertheless, these people can accept some suggestions to spiritual scanning of the self, and psychotherapy.

7. *Against Others.* This is not constantly an antisocial dimension. During spiritual counseling, this might represent an externalized spiritual conflict. For example, this subject, by neglecting his/her own spiritual needs, openly attacks others' religions, beliefs, and spirituality. Perhaps, strong ideologies and religious extremism can find a collocation in this category. Whenever these people suffer, they are sometimes ashamed of becoming "tender" and "spiritual". As a result, they might strive to constantly affirm their machismo and uncompromising ideas. It is, then, the counselors' task to gently move to the next direction of TS-AO, helping this person to autonomously find his own inner dimension, even though s/he

might not like to share it with others. Many times, extraordinary insights might come just from people who polarize their creeds, and who deny any spiritual dimension. Here, a probe question can be: "Do you feel you can make right judgments about the real intentions and spiritual life of other people?", "Do you believe that spirituality is not a subject that should be treated by 'practical people'?".

8.   *Towards the Self and Against the Others.* It is one of the most common movements during a personal growth. Here, self-development and spiritual growth do not encompass any idea of togetherness and brotherhood. Practically, spirituality is mainly self-centered, and religion can become a reason for justifying polar positions, biases, and extremism. Sometimes, this person believes that the health of the own soul is the only thing that matters. Other times, although a subject is still able to find satisfying answers to his own quest for meaning and development, this movement to self-unity is often attained at the cost of creating phantom external groups to which conflicts are projected (often creating the basis for religious intolerance). Therefore, a spiritual counselor working with these people, should be aware that this subject is willing to teach something about his/her own views instead of humbly accepting a dyadic process of development, and substantially allowing a serene basis for mutual (counselor plus client) growth and movement. Specifically, spirituality is also a feeling of connectedness and togetherness, thus, it is a "moving and feeling together". Here, probe questions about spirituality can be: "Do you believe that in some sense your personal and spiritual experience is somehow richer and deeper than that of other people?", "Do you feel that your personal meanings and spiritual understandings are closer to the Lord than the spiritual personality of your counselor?", "Do you feel closer to the Lord than any other else?". For example, in his Decalogue of Assisi For the Peace, Pope John Paul II (February 24, 2002), states: "We make efforts to talk with sincerity and patience, not considering what divides us as unsurmonting walls, but, on the contrary, acknowledging that experiencing the diversity in others can become an opportunity for a wider reciprocal understanding". The spiritual dimension as guided by social obligations is much emphasized by Jewish Talmud spirituality. For example, Samuel Belkin states that this is called democratic Jewish theocracy where, each Jewish person is responsible for the well-being of other fellows when s/he has the power for acting this way, and this is a personal obligation.[8]

Figure 1 – The star represents the directions of interpersonal relationships. We observe that during spiritual development, a person moves from purely self-centered positions (TS = Toward the Self) to more philanthropic points (TO = Toward the Others). Other intermediate sites, suggest conflicting states of mind, e.g.: AO = Against the Others. (Points: TS = Toward the Self; TS-TO = Toward the Self and the Others; TO=Toward the Others; TO-AS = Toward the Others-Against the Self; AS = Against the Self; AO-AS = Against the Others and Against the Self; AO = Against the Others; TS-AO = Towards the Self-Against the Others)

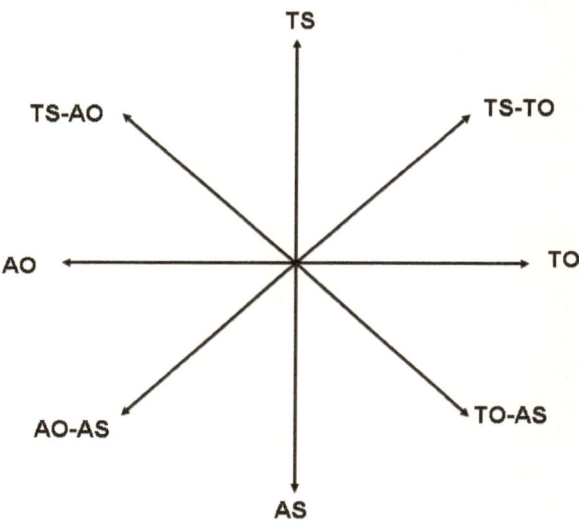

The 8 dimensions of spiritual movement during interpersonal relationships

Figure 2 – Directions in spiritual counseling. We shall find a final target in a state where a person loves both others and self (TS-TO). This shall be interpreted in a spiritual way seeing a person who acquires self-care and self-understanding through communitarian bonds, who feels morally lifted when loving others, and who increases personal well-being by promoting social development, etc.

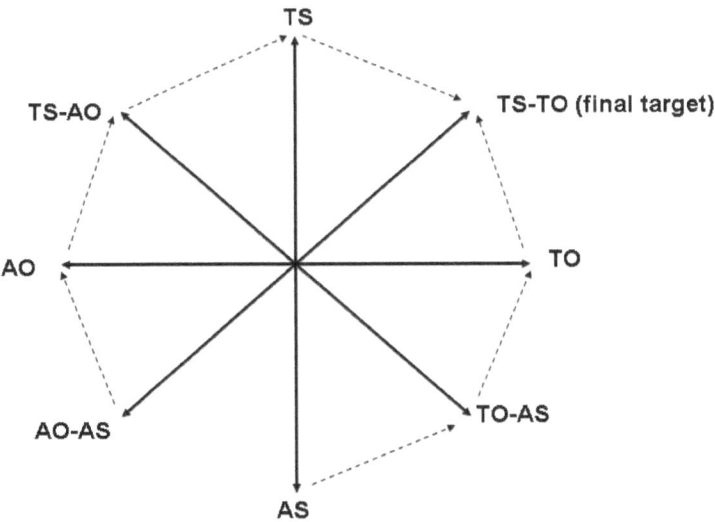

The directions in spiritual counselling (dotted arrows) and final target

1.3. SPIRITUAL COUNSELING DURING ADVERSE LIFE EVENTS

Counseling and spirituality
are both ways for the inner search.

The "meaning of life" relates to an existential as well as to a spiritual approach to counseling of people with life-threatening diseases. In the recursive thoughts and ruminations that severely ill people present, there are running topics about life that generate some core questions in their quest for a meaning. Following some of these subjects:

- Life and its meaning, now.

- Death and dying and the meaning for the self and the others. Meanings in client's spiritual relationship.

- Meaning of brotherhood and sisterhood in client's spiritual relationships.

- The vacant role after death, and what will happen to one's own role after death: profession, family, spouse.

- Emotional reactions of family and friends to client's own death.

- The destiny of one's own soul, and what is stated by religion about life after death.

- The conclusion of life and the effort to give a spiritual and human meaning to life during the last days of survival.

Usually, spiritual counselors shall be familiar with these quests for meanings, but mostly, they shall be ready to "guide clients" during (patient's self-generated) spiritual explorations of life and death. Shall the counselor be unprepared, the whole process of assistance would be jeopardized. Actually, the stress itself of being a victim of a severe disease, of unsustainable life experiences, of a violence, etc., launches all clients inside an orbit of unmatched questions: "Why me?", "Why now?", "Why the Lord is not listening to me?". Much more, during a stressful life event, it is important to meet these questions and to search for them if unspoken. Sometimes, clients are reluctant to disclose these topics because feeling that the counselor is interested only in objective data, or psychological reactions. Consequently, the whole setting of personal spirituality and metaphysic beliefs remains concealed to the most, and hardly explored. It is, thus, a counselor's task to make openings on these topics, and to send clear messages that s/he is ready to discuss about them even though s/he is not a pastor, a priest, a rabbi, etc. Furthermore, the existence in hospital of units for crises addressed to serious pathologies, where the whole team is trained to discuss about spiritual topics, makes the process of sequential encounters with patients more effective (see Fig. 3). Here, each health operator can intervene with specific skills in spiritual counseling because the whole team is trained to discuss about spiritual topics. This gives to clients an idea of continuity, and the feeling to deal with a brotherhood and not with a single "voice in the desert": each single counselor or health worker. After identifying a dynamic group, the Unit For Spiritual Counseling, clients will feel confident in discussing about spiritual matters also because they reach another goal in their spiritual growth and healing strategies: feeling to live in an extended "family". Indeed, it is important for vulnerable and sick people to get the feeling to live in a "caring context". Much because of a physiological and psychological weakness, but much more because patient's feeling of hopelessness and helplessness requires that the whole team is committed to the same client, with the same feelings, and with a "caring love". It would be stressful for a client to meet people of the same team who cure him/her according to different levels of attention: someone who is "solely" interested to his/her education, a doctor who restricts his/her intervention to check for signs of diseases, and a nurse who behave in a warm and understanding manner. Instead, the idea of connectedness and family are mutually operating in spiritual counseling. Besides, the issues treated by different people acting on each client, should be coordinated, and, if possible, sequential. In addition, in order to accept a spiritual assistance, clients must gain the idea that people who are trying to help them have the right charisma to discuss about topics concerning religion, soul, spirit, etc. For example, Peter Roche de Coppens thinks that the helper is the therapy, and that, "Much more important than techniques and clinical experience of the therapist, is just his capability to establish a *good relation* with patients, by transmitting trust, making exchanges with him/her, and *acting as therapeutic force*".[9]

Generally speaking, a spiritual counselor should be an "example" for his life, and shall provide the idea of being a "good person". This attitude conveys to clients the message that counselor's ideas, life, and spiritual understanding are coordinated. Besides, it is difficult for clients to accept any spiritual talk by someone they do not respect or that do not consider as a "good person". Much more difficult is to be convincing in spiritual subjects if counselor's life is a contradiction of what s/he "states" during counseling sections and how s/he publicly "behaves". Unfortunately, in many Italian hospitals (but also elsewhere), moral and ethical rules are infringed many times by health operators, and it is hard to start any spiritual approach to patients, or even an acceptable professional interaction. In a word, spirituality involves the whole person of a counselor, his/her way of being and behaving, his/her soul and beliefs. Actually, when a counselor starts a section or a program of spiritual counseling, a client believes that the counselor can somehow offer a model, his/her own experience, understanding, and open his/her soul. In other words, a *counselor functions as a model for each client, and partly a client will copy counselor's attitudes in order to reach higher insights.* Basically, training in spiritual counseling is also a work on counselor's transparency and trust, private and public image, ethics and attitudes, congruencies and contradictions. In addition, because spiritual counselors often talk about personal experiences and religious beliefs, religion-oriented clients, and those particularly responsive to moral issues, would seek a congruity between counselor's words and counselor's personality, accepting counselors with a correct "moral attitude" more. For example, the *charisma* of big healers, saints, and religious leaders was a basic instrument for their miracles. Similarly, without charisma, spiritual counseling risks to be vain or superficial, while a charisma itself can stay alone as a *therapeutic force.* Finally, we meet the process of trust and mistrust. Principally, a spiritual counselor shall be a trustworthy person because a charisma can be void if clients do not trust their counselors. Although there are many people who have gained the fame of being charismatic, and even though any gurus hold these positions, yet not all of them are trustworthy. In effect, *trust* reinforces charisma and gives it the "passport" for existence. Hence, if charisma is not associated to trust, clients will withdraw their consent from someone, a counselor, or other health operators that the own affiliates might still consider as charismatic or central. To conclude, charisma and trust, that are personal and moral attitudes of a counselor, are strategic, and reinforce his/her strategies of counseling and patient's compliance to counseling and therapy. In other words, there cannot be an effective spiritual counseling without making trust, charisma, and strategies congruent amongst them. Here, clients assign trust and charisma to caretakers, while the strategies belong to counselor's skills.

1.4. SPIRITUAL MOVEMENTS

> *When we fly on spiritual wings,*
> *we land on islands of*
> *multiple chances.*

The term "going to", which might seem a simple verb of movement, has truly historical and noble origins. In fact, the expression "walking", from the Italian "cammino", the Spanish "camino", and the French "chemin", finds its roots from the Sanskrit and the Old Persian, precisely from the derivation "Gam" that means "Going, Moving". Here, we shall interpret it, now as "walk" *sensu scrictu*, now as it is proposed by Honoré de Balzac, and, finally, as "Walking and Progressing" *sensu latu*. As we shall see, either in one case or in the other, we soon move from its physical indication in order to embrace philosophical, psychological, and anthropological meanings, which treat "Moving" and "Walking" as synonyms. Consequently, if we try to interpret how a spiritual movement looks like, we can refer to the theory of Honoré de Balzac, who, in his original book *Théorie de la démarche* (*The Theory of Walking*, published in Italy with the title *Teoria del Camminare*, with Sugarco, 1993) makes some statements about the word "Walking": "No expression is able, with similar immediacy, to represent life and its expression. In its biological and historical meanings, in those collectives, and much more, in those more intimate and individual images of human condition".[10] It is, thus, the aim of a spiritual counselor to establish, during any moment of his joined growth with a client, if there is some hint of internal movement, progression, and the direction of this progress. However, as I shall explain later, this spiritual advancement is not much a spinning forward of some psychological development. On the contrary, it is typically an internal growth that is similar to a recursive feedback, a sort of *circular movement*. Honoré de Balzac adds: "All participates to movement; but it shall not prevail in any direction".[11] Hence, in order to pinpoint the psychological as well as the philosophical aspects of a spiritual development, I have introduced in italics, and at the beginning of each chapter, a metaphor symbolizing some sort of spiritual movement. Moreover, a circular movement is also suggested by other Authors who compare a spiritual growth to the Hawk and the Eagle in the Native Americans: "Through Eagle, Native people are reminded of the great expanse of the universe and its circular motion of interconnectedness and interdependence, remembering always to keep the larger picture in view as they move through life. Through the Hawk, Native people are reminded of the need to remember where they are in relation to everything else, focusing neither completely on themselves nor on everything else, but rather recognizing that exists and honoring that relationship at all times".[12]

Figure 3 – In order to promote a progressive well-being during counseling in hospital, and whenever a team of specialists is intervening in the helping relation with patients, it is important to design a coordinated approach. Compared to traditional counseling, spiritual counseling prefers a synchronized and progressive approach, where each helper acts always on the same topic, along a continuum of the same subject matter.

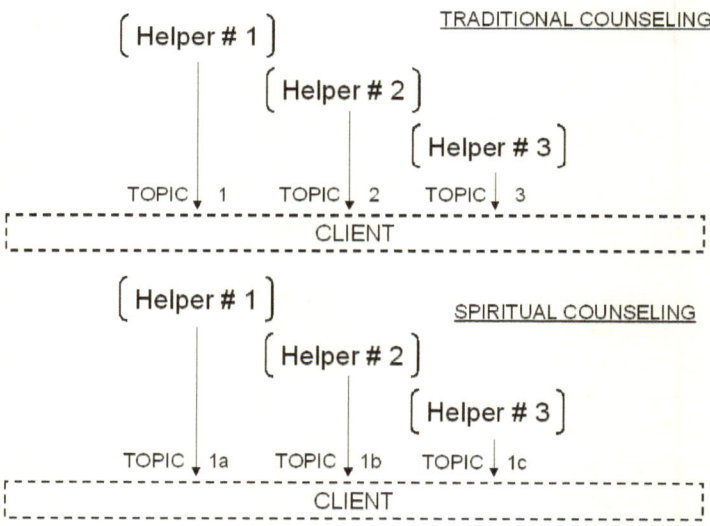

1.5. SPIRITUAL DEVELOPMENT

> *The movement of man is identifiable*
> *by progressive forward steps*
> *towards unknown and far targets,*
> *to finally land in places*
> *closer and closer to the Self.*

Usually, in our daily talk, we use as synonyms the terms "walking" and "going". In this part of the book we will use them as similar, with a slight prevalence of the over comprehensive verb "going". Practically, this last represents, at the same time, the concepts of walking, moving, progressing, and aiming to something. Thus, we shall start from some historical and literary reflections, to reach a philosophical and psychological understanding of any spiritual development. In a word, "moving" usually corresponds to the visible part of going towards, although walking cannot represent all movements. Similarly, not every kind of movement can symbolize a subjective spiritual progression. Practically, we can move by walking, by bike, by car, nevertheless we can also progress in a psychic and spiritual sense. By interpreting the symbols of walking, according to Balzac, we can understand "The personality, lifestyle, and the most secret customs of a person".[13]

Because any forward movement, and spiritual progression may present different theoretical frameworks, someone can spiritually progress without physically moving or even staying immobile (like a person in a wheelchair or in a hospital bed). On the opposite, a person can remain into a catatonic psychic peace although his body is restless and encroached by chaotic movements (like in some forms of motionless anxiety). I opened this window on spiritual progression and physical movement, because spiritual development can also manifest itself through physical behaviors and visible patterns. For example, the history of Saints recovers the importance of pilgrimage and desert visitation as the evidence of an inner turmoil or spiritual development. Moreover, spiritual pilgrimages, used to improve inner growth and spiritual improvement, hung to the time of Moses who "is sent" to the desert, not because of a personal choice, when he was in conflict with the Pharaoh. Many other prophets, living before Christ, "went" to the desert or nearby to find answers to the search of the self and spirituality. From the Acts of Apostles (*At*: 22, 21) God said to Paul: "Then He said to me: 'Go, because I'll send thou far away, amongst the pagans'". Here "going to" becomes a vocational movement. Therefore: "Walking [...] is the only way for seeking God, by leaving other human fellows, by imagining Him on a mountain, towards that sky where the step cannot become flight. This is in the Old Testament, in the Koran, in the oriental mystics".[14] Even in other cultures and religions, pilgrimage is a choice to move towards other places by leaving behind whatever is mortal. Practically, any visible spiritual journey, by means of pilgrimages, religious procession, rituals, might be the tangible sign of one's own personal effort to reinforce faith and to find those answers that chaos and crowd cannot offer.

From Tibet, the *bhikkhu (monks)* are sent in the world to make adepts. In the Catholic Church, missionaries "go" towards far away lands to carry words of hope to poor and desperate people. Even when one does not "go" according to his/her own choice, the verb "to go" develops along centuries to tell about travels, explorations, discoveries, or simply, a spiritual discovery of the Self. Therefore, as for missionaries, Buddhist monks, young adepts of the Reformed Church in South America, a "spiritual travel" is a miscellaneous movement, differentiated in the following: i) an horizontal advancement: as a physical and psychological progression in one's own life where a person revisits acquired beliefs in order to make radical changes in the own existence; ii) vertical: practically representing an inner growth and the search of a *Supreme Good*; it can be performed by developing strategies for understanding religion, spirituality, and sacred writings and to change perspective by using improved spirituality to discover "truth and the real self"; iii) a metaphysical (from Latin: "what is beyond the physical world") movement: for example, the research of deity can be achieved by reading the inner self through meditation or eremitic isolation; a person, already familiar with a religion or spiritual movement, searches for higher forms of meditation and imagination, for example through the use of sacred art; iv) circular, as a way of "going again" towards the self for a new and fresh understanding of the soul; in this case, a person's self-discovery is truly a back and forth development from physical world, to spiritual self, again to physical world. In the hypothesis of a circular spiritual movement, clients are not completely glued to a complete spiritual experience, but, at times, have moments of existential pressures because the appeals of the physical world (what is known of the world and what is physical in the world) can still attract and distract the real movement of (self)discovery.

In some way, we could parallel the movement towards a spiritual self-discovery to Victor Frankl's quest for meaning. Basically, in a dynamic existence, and in a spiritual research, questions are much more important than answers because a spiritual movement usually is not signed by a finite sense to the own life. Perhaps, this is a new ontology for the sciences of the soul, where man understands that answers are not so important like the inquiries about life. It follows that in his/her constant and historical-anthropological movement, man reinforces the idea of a forward progression with the plan of a personal spiritual growth, or as Stanard states: "Spirituality is a developmental process [...] in terms of faith development".[15] Much more, I would see a spiritual development during life events as a circular and recurrent engagement from being totally self-centered to being other-centered (Garret says: "from *being cared for* to *caring for*"[16]), from being totally inward-centered to being wholly outward-centered, from being fully focused on bodily discomforts to being completely reestablished by spiritual relief, and form being satisfied by knowledge to being unhappy about ethics in society.

In some sense, there could be no movement without creating gradients or polarizations as we have seen, with emotional loops from desperation to satisfaction. Thus, during spiritual growth, a "sacred passion" is a blend of states of internal satisfactions and dissatisfactions, passing through stages of psychic and emotional alert. Consequently, as spiritual counselors, when we meet people seeming totally "self-fulfilled", "self-actualized", "peaceful and satisfied", we shall try to "restart the psychological motor" because psycho-spiritual development is a "movement" and not a "state". And movements, as we have just told, are circular and dynamic, and not linear and progressive. Consequently, the four polar movements we have met (self vs. others, inward vs. outward, body vs. spiritual, and movement vs. satisfaction), all stay inside an embracing *circle of spiritual development*, each loop showing its own movement and staying in its own state, like the small wheels of a clock (Fig. 4).

The Way, as it is the title of the most known book of Saint Escrivà de Balaguer, is a step forward simple linear movements and a proposal for a new dimension of divine development. As Saint Escrivà states in his motto N. 580: "Humbling ask to the Lord to increase your faith. And then, with new lights you will distinguish well the difference between the ways of the world and your walking of apostle".[17] Thus, the technological man, who only reinforces an objective-goal-oriented movement, often experiences his personal discomfort during his search for existential alternatives. As a result, his/her existence is totally represented by a *motum perpetum* (perpetual movement). Practically, any movement towards the search of secular meanings really becomes an endless and paradoxical circularity like in M. C. Eschers' paintings. This is the human being forever imprisoned in his own existential geometries. Consequently, in order to give a sense to his/her own progression, "somehow moves, with the hope of going to". Nevertheless, s/he cannot sense that his development could be an obsessive repetition of historical recurrences, of many *dejà vecù*, or "already lived". Instead, any innovation of the soul is "an exercise of senses and thought, more than a movement of legs. In the slowness of the step, in the frequent stops to collect from the ground a strange and unknown object, to smell a different air, to be enchanted by a far away fire, to immerge the hand in a water stream".[18]

Here, again, the importance to rediscover the "inner movement", meant as spiritual pilgrimage, where a man joins development to reflection. However, modern man often emphasizes more a "secular progression" instead of a "spiritual contemplation", and very few times reflects about his own "path in his life". Practically, he feels as if he was born to move, to go beyond himself, and to exceed his own expectations. Moreover, he believes in the autonomy of his own evolution where the self sees the other human fellow only as complementary, but not central, for his own personal growth. Practically this increases the feelings of solitude corrupted by an obsessive recurrence where one believes to have gone forward while, instead, is experiencing the feelings of stagnation. Conversely, this kind of solitude does not match the meaning of the Latin word *solus* (sole or alone) that characterizes the spiritual movement of the *monk* (form Latin *mónos* = alone). Basically, the movement of a man who "feels" alone in his life, while believing he is moving ahead, is the same as that of a mouse who endlessly moves inside a small wheel with the illusion of an endless progression. As a conclusion, a spiritual development is also a pursuit for a new spiritual path or model to apply during the search of meanings. In fact, without a road or a pathway, spiritual inspiration and growth would have no directions. I just mention an Author who asserts: "In psychology, the road is the agent that mediates between the self and the other [...] and the absence of the road in the children's drawings is indicative of the absence of affective and social links".[19]

In addition, a psycho-spiritual movement also implies going back to one's own steps, by searching what is left behind, what we missed during our forward walk. Or, it simply embraces a standing in a self-reflecting movement that is circular because is a back-and-forth growth from old experiences to new understandings, from learning from past to coping with present and future challenges. We might also use actual spiritual insights in order to re-write our personal biography with a more acceptable and meaningful script. In truth, a circular spirituality allowing us to reconcile us with our past because we feel stronger in our current life, is a tool for psychological healing. Actually, it is not just a matter of forgetting. Instead, through a spiritual lens, also adverse and stressful life events can be reincorporated into our own biography in order to use our past scars as a solid plateau for building our new life. It is curious to find that popular understanding of psychological healing is that a counselor should help the own client's suffering disappear, painful past experiences being forgotten, pleasant present conditions being reinforced, and fear of emptiness and death being discouraged.

Figure 4 –Spiritual development and the focus of spiritual counseling are circular and dynamic. This means that through several steps, a person can go back many times to initial positions, by reviewing and perfectioning them. Furthermore, the main four forces of spiritual progression (self/others; inward/outward; body/spiritual, and satisfaction/movement) are interrelated like a sort of cogwheel. For example, a person who is moving from a self-centered condition due to stress (inward), to a more community-oriented plane (outward), can also reposition the cogwheel of satisfaction/movement in order to reach a higher dynamic state of mind. This, at the same time, moves the cogwheel of spiritual/body, towards a higher degree of moral complexity, which, at the same time, rotates the cogwheel of self/others towards "others", and thus, to community. Other times, the cogwheels move independently, and according to the stage of spiritual development, a person can rotate one or more cogwheels.

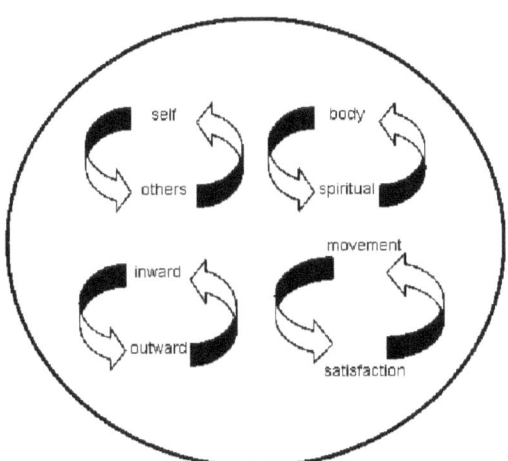

Circles of spiritual development

Basically, spiritual counseling should indeed take anything from life to transform it into the seed for internal renovation. It is a matter of seeing differently before being different. And if a child, a woman, a sick person, are helped to reconcile with their own past experiences, and to consider even painful experiences as "valuable tools" for a religious shift, then, a process of spiritual healing can develop rapidly. In other words, the task of a spiritual counselor is the promotion of client's reconciliation with the self and not the proposal of a psychological anesthesia. This portion of counseling would thus assume some milestones in the helping relationship with clients, for what concerns past experiences (in capitals "Be" propositions):

- "Be yourself". Which means: "Be the manager of yourself".

- "Your past life should not be condemned but used as a starting point for reflection and spiritual growth". Which stays for: "Be positive about yourself and do not accept to condemn yourself".

- "Have an eagle watch on past experiences. Do not stick on them as if they were the only responsible of what you are today". Here, we can say: "Keep moving and do not justify your stops by indulging with thoughts about your past".

- "What have you learned from past experiences that you find valuable today?". In a statement: "Please, consider yourself as a rich person because of the positive as well as negative experiences you made in your past life".

- "Will you be able to tell to yourself: 'Stop!' when trying to justify your present weaknesses as if they were the logical heritage of your past?". In a statement: "In order to be totally spiritual, you should search for alternative ways of living and thinking without regressing to old shelters".

- "Are you willing to make a commitment to your own spiritual growth by considering yourself as a man (or a woman) of yourself instead of incriminating what has been done to you, told to you, and taken from you in the past?". In a statement: "There is something wonderful that nobody will ever take away from you: you belong to yourself".

- "Well, being spiritual also means to consider yourself as a wonderful person also as a result of what you have been or not been in your past". Say aloud: "Thank you 'past', for what I am 'now', and what I will be 'tomorrow'".

This process of *reconciliation with the own past* is particularly significant with underprivileged and violated children, and youngsters undertaking rehabilitation programs. For example, people who were particularly unlucky in their childhood or later on, shall move, as soon as possible, towards a reconciliation process before they can move further in their spiritual growth. Otherwise, they may use spirituality not as an instrument for growth but as a way "to forget". Practically, although a tendency to forget the injustices received is partly central to many religious thoughts, in spiritual counseling it acquires a different meaning. It is not meant as a "lack of memory" but as a reshaping of past experiences in other to use them as resources. Thus, a violated child does not tell to himself: "I shall forget my father who was violent with me", but "I can use this experience to learn how to be a better person". This process of reconciliation gives back the responsibility for growth to the person itself who, encouraged and protected by the counseling setting, will chose in what amount to dip from past incidents for picking up "meaningful experiences", even though their were painful. In some extent, if life is a continuous learning, then we learn from positive as well as from negative events. Thus, by matching black and white zones of our life we get the meaningful gray in the between. In conclusion, self-pity is not a way of considering spiritual progress.

So far, as we have been seeing, a spiritual movement is a sort of *re*-flection or circular movement, which presents recurring loops. Practically, the Self explores its own territories, and, at the same time, moves externally to pursue connectedness with other human beings. For example, for Jung the circle is a "representation of the self".[20] The Celtic Cross showing a circle that is lying on a cross symbolically represents this concept of circular movement. Furthermore, the value of circularity, that in the Catholic Religion is mainly symbolized by the necklace of the Saint Rosary, reminds us how important is for a spiritual development the repetition and the rituality of the subject who meditates. This is the same circularity and repetition of the Ohm of Buddhist Monks or of Cappadocic dancers. For the last ones, this is a ceremony used in the practice of Sufism in order to reach the ecstatic link with the divine through the *sema* (listening). During this ceremony, characterized by prayer, music, and dance, the prayer-dancer reaches the *wajd* (state of trance) consisting in the inspiration and the revelation of truth. The *sema* of Mevlevi dervish groups is achieved by the whirling Dervish who dance accompanied by instrumental and vocal music, waiting the trance. For example, Honoré de Balzac, reminds us that grace is characterized by "rounded forms"[21], therefore, emphasizing that a man who is harmony with the self and the Universe, somehow copies these movements by reproducing the orbital dances of planets.

The introduction at the importance of a circle in the geometry of life is attributed to the Pythagoreans who identified in the *olkos*, upholding, the force that was ruling the Universe and influencing the constant recurrence of seasons, the movement of asters, and the cycle of life. In the circumference, according to Pythagoreans, any beginning becomes end, and vice versa, any end becomes beginning.

In the Christian architecture, the main domes in the churches are always circular, this recalling the main circularity of any spiritual movement of soul, life, death, resurrection to which any believer is linked. Furthermore, the frescoes in the walls of the main domes often report choirs of angels. As some Authors point out: "The Oriental tradition uses the circle to represent the cycle of reincarnations. The numerous roses that decorate the sacred monuments are part of the same symbolism and are one of the symbols of the divine unity. The unity is also represented in the *round dance,* that is the expression of brotherhood, of the human chain, of the strength of the love through union".[22] Thus, a circular movement, and the circle that represents it, are the return, the reflection, the way in which a man and a woman, in their efforts to spiritually progress, come back to wonder about themselves, by transforming their existences into a virtuous circle of collective movement. "This way a man puts at its finger a ring, the spiritual one, which reminds him about his faith, his commitment to connectedness with others and with God".[23]

The final virtual circle (Fig. 5) links the Three Spiritual Routes (the 3 Fs) to Connectedness with Others: Forgetting, Forgiving, Forthcoming: i) "Forgetting" means avoiding to mentally indulge on past social negative experiences; ii) "Forgiving" means canceling the hatred and the feelings of revenge about unfortunate social experiences; iii) "Forthcoming" means being always other-oriented during social relationships, by being cooperating, accommodating, and available. Although during existential crises, even if not directly linked to social deeds, people like to feel that somebody else is responsible for their personal suffering, this external locus of control is germane to the spiritual growth, and should be weakened in clients by proposing them the virtual circle of connectedness. Occasionally, people consider themselves as responsible and guilty for their actual existential difficulties and anguishes, and also in this occasion, the process of reconciliation is addressed to the self.

1.6. ANTHROPOLOGY OF SPIRITUALITY TO COPE WITH MISFORTUNE

When we are desperate
and unable to progress,
we look for alternative and inner routes
for changing the way we move in the world.

A man who lives totally the drama of impasse and desperation, also experiences the no-movement, the no-progress, the no-future. Here, each movement becomes, indeed, a desperate appeal to "go away" for the search of improbable places of well-being, only to fall again in a repetitive social drama, in another unsatisfying social relationship, work, alternative cure, slum, prison. The misfortune of a human being who stops his/her spiritual progression, becomes even more strident when compared to the development of a person who can dream, who is involved in healing, who has the tangible feeling that s/he can still have opportunities and future. Moreover, for the underprivileged person, socially deprived, there is also a cognitive impasse, and his personal dictionary often fails in showing verbal expressions about future and movement. Nevertheless, it is often during these adversities that people get some extra energy to make some progression in their spirituality and faith. For example, in order to understand and study this development, narrative researches onto the accounts that people give, are suggested as one of the courses that the investigators should follow for understanding the meaning that people give to life.[24] In addition, according to some Authors, there are 4 patters of moving towards spiritual growth in patients with serious illnesses: "(1) the Deferring Believer ('God allows things to happen for a reason.'); (2) the Collaborating Believer ('This is where I'm supposed to be.'); (3) the Religious/Spiritual Seeker ('I'm trying to get my life together.'); and (4) the Self-Directing Believer ('What else is new?')".[25]

A person facing desperation and misfortune has, thus, only one way to develop and to move: spiritually transforming the plight in his/her life. For example, street children and their poor parents in South America lack, cognitively, verbal expressions to quantify the breadth of "going" and the significance of "future". Much more, the same jargon language used by children and youngsters to communicate with their peers, encage them into the use of present tenses, as they state: "Tomorrow you do not know if you are still alive". Their parents reveal the same cognitive frameworks. In addition, the physical, existential, and developmental stop is much more strident in the juvenile jails in South America. Here, children loose their grasp to life, deprived of any existential safety in a violent environment.[26]

Figure 5 – The spiritual routes to connectedness with self and others, and their virtuous circle. Each apex of the triangle indicates that the achieved condition is not prominent over the others. Moreover, the circularity indicates that each position is touched and reviewed along any loop, which means that a person can cross and meliorate any position many times during the own spiritual development. In addition, during each loop, there is also a progressive forward push to the next step, indicating that the achievement in one-step (forgiving, forgetting, and forthcoming) determines an enhancement of the next station. For example, a person who is forgetting the suffered wrongs, is also forgiving more the wrong doers. Alternatively, a person who is forgiving more through prayer, is also more forgetting of the suffered wrongs. Finally, those who are more forthcoming, tend to forgive more or to forget more. Etc. The loop can go clockwise or in the opposite direction. These loops function either towards the others or towards the self. For example, a person who is accepting the self more (forgiving), is much more oriented to forget negative past experiences caused by other people.

FORGETTING

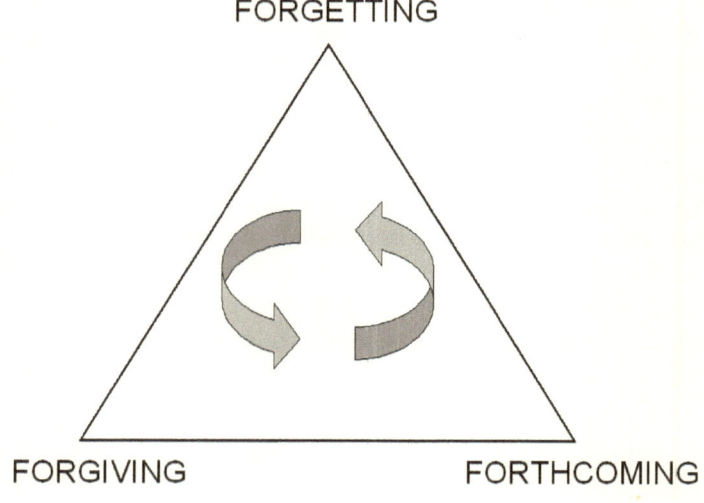

FORGIVING   FORTHCOMING

During the period when I was a missionary psychologist in developing countries, I met villages that were growing "on" and around garbage deposits. Here, the life of millions of people is engulfed by an endless and desperate survival, fed only by what they can get from garbage disposals. Thus, food deprivation, malnourishment, communicable diseases weaken the survival spirit of human beings living in the garbage cities in many developing countries. In these places, the concept of personal development and "going" seems apparently blocked, while, apparently, it is possible only to recede physically, or partially regress to a sort of aboulic acceptance of the Earth Jeenna. This last was simply the garbage deposit out of the walls of Jerusalem where rubbish was usually incinerated. Actually, in many poor countries, a similar scenario can be found where people live on and around garbage deposits. Here, adults and children collect recyclable rubbish.

However, in these places, the effort to live and to be, is a big achievement in order to win the strong aspiration to not being. Nonetheless, spiritual experiences here are visible and constant. In these places, local churches, Pentecostal experiences, and Catholic missionary's schools find reliable and sensible people. Through spiritual awareness, religious services, prayers, and group congregations these people have found the instruments to live where life is a constant bet. But, not everyone is so lucky. Poverty of values embraces happy islands of renewed spiritual growth and faith. And, side-by-side to churches, in these desperate villages, we find places of perdition.

1.7. THE EXPERIENCE OF STASIS AND EXISTENTIAL IMPASSE

> *In order to stop falling when walking,*
> *we seek alternative and safer routes*
> *inside the mazes of our Self.*

Feeling of stasis and existential impasse are the tyranny for our life projects. Nevertheless, if we look at a man in his resilience and capability to progress, if we consider other dimensions, more vertical, or spiritual, then life kinetics and values change. In order not to "fall" –as the cultural anthropology leads man to reinforce his/her own resilience instead of weaken it up– a human being wonders about alternative routes that his/her walking can assume. For example, by living in a psychic and physical space of a three-dimensional kind: with: i) a horizontal axis x which is the *interpersonal and social* movement; ii) a perpendicular axis y which is the *biological and bio-*

somatic movement; and, iii) a vertical axis *z* which is the *spiritual* movement. An integrated approach to human growth shall thus consider the three dimensions as equally important, while a spiritual counselor shall be aware of the neat prevalence of one over the others. In this sense, there is also a mutual and positive influence amongst configurations: spirituality can help interpersonal skills but also has effects on physical health. The concern of some psychiatrist of seeing spirituality as reinforcement of depressive helplessness and hopelessness, leading to externalize locus of control shall also be taken into account. Neither can an integrated psychic growth be separated by the importance of body health (axis *y*), and of social relationships (axis *x*). Sometimes, weakness in the investment or activation in one axis (for example, momentary or prolonged disease), leads to reinforce alternative axes: social interactions, spiritual growth, and faith. On the same hand, prolonged and forcible isolation from a social network (e.g., jail, forced confinement, hospitalization) can strengthen religious beliefs and faith. What happens when it is the spiritual axis that is suffering? By some means, the same. People might invest in body health (promoting a good stamina or obsessive medical check-ups) as the only discipline that seems giving them protection from (the fear of) diseases, or indulge in groupies and club affiliation to avoid the solitude of the Self.

According to this renewed geometry, a person who is seriously unwell, bed ridden, who enjoys the reading of sacred writings, reaches some compensatory life satisfaction while having secular meanings blocked. If spirituality can be thus treated as a way standing by itself, that self-suffices and helps people to cope with difficult life events, and if a spiritual movement is what is visible to counselors, then any other alternative "movement" and sense making can apparently be a parachute from feelings of falling in the emptiness. Therefore, this transformed existential kinetics might shed new light to known ways of interpreting inner movements. On the other hand, alternative sense-making efforts, when not spiritual, can be temporary resorts to existential hurdles, all blossoming from reinforcement of the two lefts axes: social or bio-somatic. Besides, a spiritual counselor shall not make moral judgments. Actually, the diagnostic tools s/he has to interpret personal well-being of clients is to establish if sense-making strategies are robust barriers to crises or vulnerable and temporary defenses: e.g., many people after a diagnosis of a serious disease, start strict vegetarian diets (bio-somatic axis) or stop staying alone (social axis). Nevertheless, a spiritual movement is, as already stated, an integration of the three (spiritual, social, bio-somatic) harmonized dimensions. For example, Honoré de Balzac underlines the importance of living according to synchronized movements: "A human movement is accomplished according to well identifiable moments. If you confuse them you obtain a mechanic rigidity".[27]

The same fluid and synchronized development shall be then observed or promoted during spiritual counseling, just by monitoring if social or bio-somatic movements are prevailing. For example, if a client is at the moment unable to locate himself inside the right coordinates, then a counselor shall think about periods of immersion inside one and only one axis at the time, by allowing extra benefits from alternative growths. For instance, after a period of behavioral therapy because of an unbalanced diet, a diabetic client shall move onto frequent social encounters in order to reinforce the feeling of being loved and cared; as a secondary result s/he can then accept diet restrictions and counselor's warnings. Finally, a spiritual development can be introduced also as ancillary to the two (social and biological), benefiting from a better body health and social network. This represents a *dynamic spiritual counseling*. Apparently, this is slight different from enforcing the client inside a rigid jacket of spiritual-social-body remedies. Instead, *as a patron of the total client's well-being, a counselor shall equally address social, body, and spiritual health and development of clients*. In a word, a total person is a spiritual, physical and social being. And, as Balzac stated: "movement shall not prevail in any direction".[28]

Finally, as in any psychotherapeutic contract, a counselor shall clarify what will be a visible and a viable solution a client wants to achieve by presenting to counseling sections. Basically, visible solutions are clear behavioral and practical achievements that anyone can see and appreciate. Viable solutions are, indeed, an attempt to avoid that during contract agreement a client and a counselor accept unattainable and unreliable goals: "Being a good person", "Reaching God", "Being what I never was", and so on. Particular attention should, thus, be paid especially in spiritual counseling, where there can be a mix of too much spirituality and Heaven leading to "airy" and "light-hearted" counseling interventions.

Figure 6 – The tridimensional (static) model of existential development

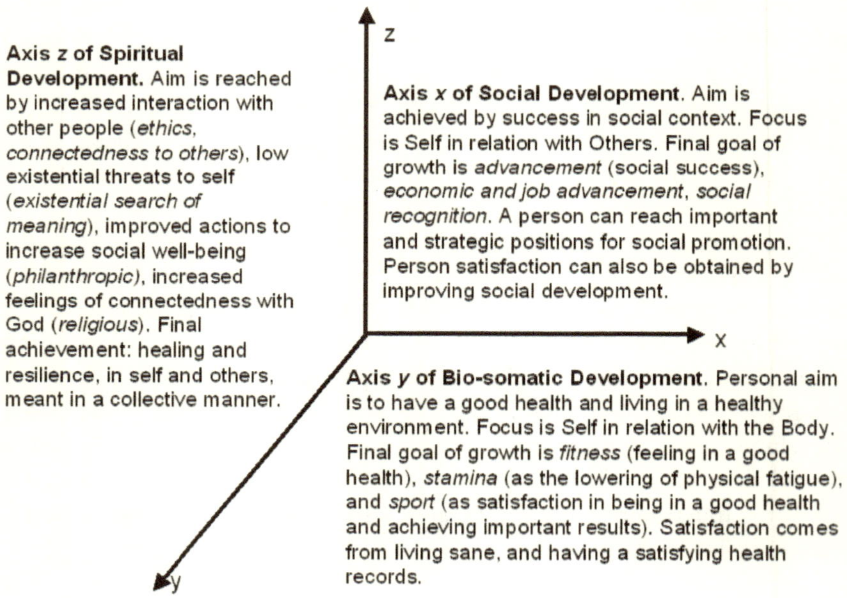

Axis z of Spiritual Development. Aim is reached by increased interaction with other people (*ethics, connectedness to others*), low existential threats to self (*existential search of meaning*), improved actions to increase social well-being (*philanthropic*), increased feelings of connectedness with God (*religious*). Final achievement: healing and resilience, in self and others, meant in a collective manner.

Axis x of Social Development. Aim is achieved by success in social context. Focus is Self in relation with Others. Final goal of growth is *advancement* (social success), *economic and job advancement, social recognition*. A person can reach important and strategic positions for social promotion. Person satisfaction can also be obtained by improving social development.

Axis y of Bio-somatic Development. Personal aim is to have a good health and living in a healthy environment. Focus is Self in relation with the Body. Final goal of growth is *fitness* (feeling in a good health), *stamina* (as the lowering of physical fatigue), and *sport* (as satisfaction in being in a good health and achieving important results). Satisfaction comes from living sane, and having a satisfying health records.

Figure 7 – A dynamic model for spiritual development and counseling. This virtuous circle partly indicates that spiritual development and counseling are also progressive forward movements of both physical health and social development. Moreover, each point of the circle can alternatively become a starter for the next stages. For example, a progressive spiritual development of a person will conduct to a higher inclination and attention to social issues and feelings of bond with brothers and sisters. This increases a personal well-being, which will enhance the perception of physical health. By experiencing this renewed force, a person further develops a deeper spiritual interest and understanding, which also increases social strategies for making bonds with other human beings. Naturally, counselors can promote all these stages as a strategy for healing and health of their clients. The whole process is also dynamic and implies a constant and progressive development of bio-somatic, spiritual, and social skills.

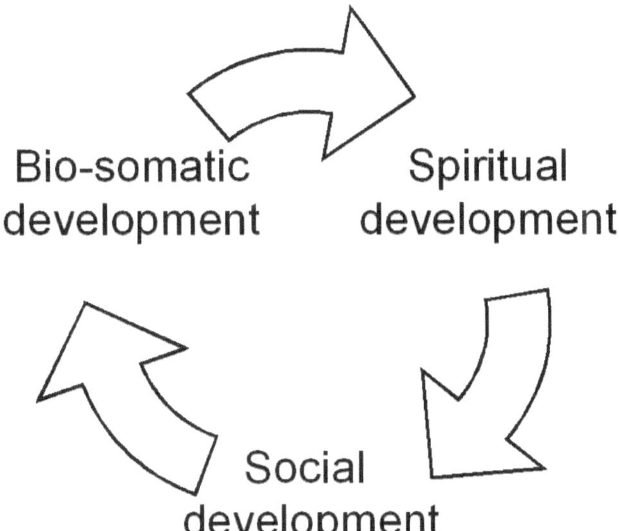

Bio-somatic development

Spiritual development

Social development

1.8. A DIFFERENT GEOMETRY OF HUMAN PROGRESSION

> *When we cannot distinguish*
> *a clear route anymore,*
> *we change our inner*
> *point of observation.*

A different cultural anthropology and the valorization of a spiritual growth would create a different social value system for the definition of well-being. For example, very poor people might then show higher resilience when compared to wealthy people. Consequently, a tridimensional psychic geometry would rearrange social statuses making full of resources, and a remarkable point of observation, precisely those social strata that use spirituality as their core strategy for survival. For example, multi-denominational churches appearing in South America, and the massive participation to ceremonies of underprivileged social classes, would reinforce the idea that church participation, communitarian prayers, and spiritual growth, are the privileged avenues to survival and increased existential resilience for those who have no access to alternative sources of well-being: education, wealth, work, health, and nutrition.

Another striking aspect of any spiritual movement is the communitarian participation. Whenever spirituality is claimed to be central to personal growth, a communitarian co-movement towards this goal is found. In addition, participation to ecumenical movements becomes a way to acquire courage.[29] In fact, Prof. Klausner states that society develops instrument of infusion of courage and faith, and this is achieved through the participation to communitarian worshiping in religious institutions.[30] In addition, according to Klausner participation to group worshiping and to religious ceremonies is a strategy that people use in order to reduce existential anxiety.[31] We can, thus, assume that this differential value system, with its norms, obligations, and focuses would change also the social interpretation and definitions of well-being, progress, and success.

Practically, we would assist to a cognitive restyling, positioning a psychological well-being right on mutual support, mass participation, communitarian prayer, pilgrimages, chaplain support of college students, and so forth. Here, too, a personal focus would move from a self-centered perspective –which corresponds to a historical reinforcement of social and psychological habits usually addressed to the individual per se– to a more group-centered standpoint. This "spiritual renovation" would correspond to a new psychological movement emphasizing a social-spiritual "intelligence" as capability to interact with others and as a way to achieve personal satisfaction and well-being. For example, if we go back to the philosophy of "going", Prof. Duccio Demetrio declares: "Who will not desire that those anonymous and symptomatic walks 'all for himself', would indeed sometime become a 'walking with'?".[32]

Basically, this progressive interest in spiritual and social "intelligence" would alternatively stress a new psychological semeiotic also for reading verbal and non-verbal communication according to spirituality. For example, how can we distinguish those who are already using spirituality as a life motif for increasing resilience? How would a counselor test spirituality in his/her clients? What are the new value system and the new vocabulary in interpersonal relationships between helpers and clients, "both" adhering to a regimen of spiritual understanding? And much more: "What are the new pathologies that can be diagnosed by a spiritual counselor?". For instance, if we focus on some expressions that are becoming a form of slogan for deciphering personal discomfort, we start to witness some recurrent claims: "value emptiness", "lack of solidarity", "fear of abandonment", and so on. These are the new symptoms reported by "spiritual clients". Moreover, the existence of a personal suffering created by the presence of a disease, anxiety, crisis, would accentuate these spiritual discomforts. From here, we can hypothesize new existential worries: i) the fear to fall for lack of support, recommendations, and patronization; ii) the fear to live in a social context where it is difficult to share the same value and spiritual system; iii) the anxiety to be pressed to adhere to undesired goals at work or in family; iv) the stress for having the own life ruled by people apparently with no ethical inclination; iv) the dread to conceal the own religious creed and religious intolerance; v) etc. For example, as the philosopher Bianca Maria Ventura states: "The common sense of progressing and moving makes people to seek for a personal "patron" to ovoid the risk of precipitating".[33]

In conclusion, according to this renovated kinetics of personal and spiritual growth, the definitions of existential movement change. For example, the movement is meliorated in delay, success with hiding, living forever in living for others. As an Author states: "This vertical vision is spiritual and social. Overcoming one's own personal condition means to evolve from the base to the vertex. By doing this man evolves not only from the bottom to the height, but progresses going from quantity (width of the basis) to quality (narrowness of the vertex)".[34]

1.9. KINET(H)IC MODELS OF MOVEMENT

Disarticulated and
diskinetic movements
of our walking
appear when we experience
our limited worlds
and feel entrapped in them.

According to a renovated kinetic and ethical model (that we can name kin-*ethical*) of personal growth, people can make experience of several ways of loss of movement and fear to fall. For example, during progressive losses (health, wealth, spiritual consciousness), a person experiences the fear of falling and comes across the perception of an abyss. Here, the semeiotics of spiritual weakness emerges with particular fears, most with a sense of emptiness and existential dizziness. Sometimes, a person fills an impression of meaninglessness with fantastic creations. The attempt is to provide the Self with a false perception of movement when a person is indeed still. Furthermore, our culture, itself, at the search of a definite and restoring movement, proposes its own simulacra as fashions, tendencies, myths, and ideologies. At times, the more the spiritual progression is frail, and certainties are shaky, the more alternative spiritual simulacra appear on the scene in order to give us the false perception of movement.

Practically, there are fashions and trends also for substitutive simulacra, like the "success" as a care for our feelings of emptiness. The same perception of achieving our social and standard goals apparently reinforces our feelings of spinning, this last becoming a substitute for our perception of movement and progression. On the whole, there are *Symbolic and Substitutive Dynamic Images* (S.S.D.I.) like "success", "beauty", "wealth", but also "health" or "fitness" that stand as surrogates for the idea of movement forward. However, there are also *Symbolic and Substitutive Static Images* (S.S.S.I.) where symbols for personal progression are substituted by images of "calmness" and "rest" in order to give us the perception that even when we are still, we are indeed in a spiritual motion by sparing energy. Basically, this is found in the fashion of spirituality proposed by proponents of "relaxation" and "contact with nature" as aids to reach spirituality. Actually, there is an infinite number of proposals and books that teach meditation and relaxation as pathways to spirituality, although, sometimes lacking in clear definitions of spirituality itself. The risk is to believe that there are as many spiritual aspects as are the proponents for spiritual renovation. However, the prevailing trend is to propose calmness and rest as spiritual behaviors leading to meditation and, "therefore", to spirituality. On the other hand, always according to these shared spiritual theories, "activity and activism", are related to chaos, and, "therefore" intended as foreign to a spiritual growth.

This model, historically wants to challenge the mainstream idea of industrial and pre-industrial society. Here, "inactivity" is supposed to be a poison for mind because equal to sloth. For example, Honoré De Balzac, states: "Passivity produces lesions in the moral organism".[35] Conversely, our post-industrial culture has reaffirmed the importance of calmness and rest, as recovery strategies for the spirit. Furthermore, an over-evaluation of these biases risks to accept as true the idea that spirituality can be only reached through inactivity because close to calmness. However, this constraint, applied to a dynamic spiritual mind, might slow down any speculative and turbulent quests for spirituality, and would finally link a spiritual mind to no mind at all.

Indeed, a spiritual dimension is, instead, a "restless" and "dynamic" process that moves humanity forward, and shakes biases and culture. In addition, a spiritual and a mystical growth always demand a commitment to a restless movement of the Self. This is why we shall not confuse peace with spirituality, calmness with monastery, search of silence and spiritual growth with mental inactivity. On the whole, these are common simulacra, images of distant monks and cultures. Basically, our prepackaged culture occasionally makes unexpected conclusions about spirituality, and habitually presents us images that an opinion leader reveals as spirituality. The observer, then, follows these procedures, and recalls those sweet metaphors as truly representing spirituality. In addition, spiritual metaphors also play a heavy role in mixing the true spiritual themes with more secular ones. For example, the popular use of beautiful flowers, trees, smiling people to represent spirituality have made those metaphors accepted as "being spiritual" or "meaning spiritual". Nonetheless, the use of metaphors can anyhow be risky in treating something that usually is a personal and intangible dimension. Basically, our mainstream culture, through the excess of symbolism and metaphors, is altering the understanding of any real spiritual movement. Consequently, for a sort of sympathy, we move the same way when interpreting the allegory for spirituality, because we rather like to be in tune with other people's images instead of questioning them and to spiritually move in our own way. As Balzac comments: "Civilization [...] alters also movement".[36]

This is why spiritual growth and spiritual movement are not instinctive. For a sort of collective companionship, some people adjust their inner quest to what they imagine their neighbors are doing. Occasionally, a collective interpretation of spirituality comes from the sharing of the same metaphors and interpretations. When, then, we translate all this in counseling, we shall be prepared to meet people who are not aware that much of their personal discomfort and pain is indeed given by their difficulty to give up shared meanings and metaphors to start a more personal and independent growth. Consequently, the own suffering is personally interpreted, during counseling sections of these people, as feeling too far from the shared model that is culturally accepted as source of happiness. Here, the fragile (and unproductive) effort is to acquire with the help of a counselor enough coping strategies to restore the forces to reach those models. Instead, the counselor's proposal to substitute those secular models or to embrace no-models at all is scarcely logic in client's mind. Even more complicated is to recommend to clients some frame of analysis that is spiritual and based on the self. However, those clients who truly decide to walk to healing, also become more spiritual or, at least, start to think that spirituality is an alternative, often the only option, or a substitutive stance to interpret the Self and the others. Thus, spirituality can also become a lens by which client reinterprets happiness and calmness. As secondary gain, and in a short period, they will be able to find operational applications of spiritual understanding. Finally, through this discovery, also personal kinetics changes, and the spiritualized client "moves" more naturally, with own rhythms and relationships with others, self, and nature.

1.10. LOOKING FOR NEW SUBJECTIVE DIMENSIONS WHEN LIFE EXPECTATION IS LIMITED

> *Only through the labyrinth of the Self,*
> *mankind can achieve the perception*
> *of moving also if life is blocked.*

Body and psyche, each time, invent new ways to redefine the sense of inner advancement, especially when personal development is limited because of physical, social, and personal limitations. For example, for people living in limited spaces, on wheelchairs, in jails, in a hospital bed, in a *favela* (urban slum) the striking effort to achieve a feeling of growth and strength prevails over any other dream. Much more this happens when the perception of immobility is joined to the feeling of restriction. In a certain way, the restoration of feelings of progression, through enhanced spirituality and faith, changes the geography of any subjective development.

Consequently, a person who is physically limited, a patient during hospitalization, all seek alternatives outside the narrow limits of their body to retrieve a feeling of personal freedom and inner strength. Nonetheless, this choice usually depends on the subjective culture and experience. For that reason, the proposal of a spiritual counseling to strengthen a patient's feeling of inner growth and strength, can be seen also as an ethical alternative that nurses, doctors, and other health operators can offer to patients who feel that this can be helpful. As emphasized in this book, during palliative care, a counselor should always keep in mind that operational counseling is a social dimension conducted either in the dyad therapist-client, or in the group helper-clients. Besides, health operators shall bear in mind the added value of spirituality as an altruistic and anthropological dimension.

As a result, spiritual counseling in palliative care shall always aim to increase socialization and social bonds of clients, primarily to overcome conditions or feelings of isolation and abandonment, but also because patients like to feel still helpful to other people. This is even more important during moments of existential stresses or losses, where a progressive paucity in social life is a constant. Thus, being between others and feeling useful to others are an existential therapy that maintains its priority during diseases and progressive physical impairments. Here, self and others melt in a collective movement and in a cooperative sharing of meanings and spirituality. The end result is the reinforcement of mutual feelings of plenitude and achievement.

1.11. THE CHOICE OF A DIFFERENT SOCIAL PARADIGM

Through the experience of Love,
a sudden stop of a movement
becomes, instead, a
renewed movement of evolution.

There is no alternative way to separate the meaning of life from any prevailing social paradigm. From any observational point, the choice of a patient to participate to a spiritual development and to research alternative existential meanings, depends on his/her attitude towards the prevailing social ethics and cultural paradigms. Sometimes, society and common sense are practically empty spaces that accept any meaning till the point that no value is prevailing. Paradoxically, this also influences the theory of life development to the point that any common explanation about "growth and development" is felt, by a suffering person, as a tumble with no net. Consequently, emptiness in reassuring existential values would directly be translated into a sense of personal deprivation, and into a movement with no direction. This justifies what Victor Frankl defines the "noogenic frustrations that derive from the frustration of the craving for meaning, and from the [...] existential frustration or existential emptiness".[37]

In this case, the only anchorage that a patient can use to avoid a secure breakdown is the love and care that s/he can receive from his helper also acting as spiritual trainer. This way, a spiritual counseling similarly becomes a preferential instrument for increasing resilience in the underprivileged and miserable human beings. Here, the aim is to foster a sense of "inner growth and development" while, apparently, life shows impediments and sequential stops. Consequently, in the "blocked-up man", with the face down for embarrassment, bare foot, with blister and lumps, that has never known life and that seems living solely by a simple inertial force, we might indeed find strong potentials for the own existential and spiritual survival. Practically, the last man on the Earth is, indeed, frequently a believer, generous through nothing, stimulated by a strong religious and spiritual soul. He is disciple of the own Gods as the most devoted child.

Thus, believer. Generous while having nothing. Animated by a strong spirituality. Devotional to the Lord as the fondest between the children. Dedicated to the family as the most generous between the fathers. And, yet he dies of starvation, as frequently happens in many poor countries where people live by recycling litter! It is again the vertical dimension that is opened to whom sees its personal borders blocked by space and poverty. Here, the vertical or spiritual growth becomes the prevailing lifeboat in a man with several dimensions, and the only way for the "*desperate people*" on the Earth. Spirituality becomes, thus, a diaphanous movement that escapes from those who look at the garbage pickers in the mega cities of developing countries. However, when turning the glance at the various Religious Congregations who rise in such slums, one becomes aware of the strong spiritual needs and coping strategies of people who seek resilience into an adverse environment. Moreover, the faith in the after-life, and the aspiration to see the self as a thing gifted with value, are undeniable in people who sit in to worship with hands dirty of garbage and daily humiliations.

Basically, the spiritual need, since need, then, can become a physiological process, as it can be thirst, hunger, or the wish to exist. In short, spirituality, right in the slums of the dumps I have visited, is a demand stronger than hunger and thirst. Here, the women who discuss about the Bible in the social centers in the evening, the boys who gather in the few soccer fields of the schools inside the *slums*, all perceive a renovated life, and return to a tangible perception of a personal worth through the nourishment and reinforcement achieved from their own spirituality, faith, and worship. Thus, although they have a short existential expectancy, the inner self is not endangered and the emotional life can still have a perspective. Practically, the holistic person can reach a spiritual growth through different venues and by developing a multiple perspective in his/her spiritual existence. The anchorage to a safer version of the own existence can be reached, then, through a differential perspective about sources for the own spiritual development. Some suggestions can be collected by the writings of John White who differentiates amongst different levels of spirituality, some of which are:[38]

- "In *psychological* terms, spirituality means discovering inside the self the origin of the supreme happiness, that is, love".
- "In *sociological* terms, spirituality means to help other people in an unselfish way".
- "In *cosmological* terms, means to feel one thing with the universe, in harmony with the infinite, with the Tao".
- "In *theological* terms, is to see God in every thing, in all events, circumstances, as an infinite light of unconditional love".
- "In *ecological* terms is to pay respect for all the forms of life: vegetal, animal, human, spiritual, and angelic".

1.12. THE CIRCULAR MOVEMENT AND THE RE-DISCOVERY OF THE SELF

There is nothing painful in my life.
Everything makes me grow.

As we have been seeing, spirituality is not much a strategy to move along a straight direction with no opportunity to reinforce previous existential experiences. Moreover, although learning is always a paramount for any human development, this does not mean that we cannot learn from experience or return to our previous discoveries for promoting further growth. Similarly, recurrence applies to spiritual development and growth, to the point that it can be imagined as a circular movement on a straight line like it is the one we observe of a tire along a road. The roads, the straight line, all symbolize a long-term project and our existential goals, while the rotating movement represents what we usually do with our ego along this pathway. For example, while we aim to reach an important professional position, we can "reflect" about our past experiences, return to our previous "emotional" skills, resort our spiritual and inner achievements, and finally reposition what happens today onto what we have learned about ourselves yesterday. Practically, we use our past inner and spiritual resources to find convenient strategies for coping today. Without a historical and spiritual memory, we would basically live under a constant emotional turmoil and value emptiness. Instead, also with the help of spiritual counseling, by giving continuity to our spiritual and emotional identity, we always grow, even by recollecting past omissions and reshaping them for their hidden (spiritual) denotations. To these processes we can give name of "*Rehearsing*".

Consequently, we shall imagine that a spiritual growth related to strategies of coping and resilience during sufferings and diseases, is also a recollection of previous and similar experiences in order to place them inside a frame of significance and meaning. For instance, if a person has suffered from a loss in the past but is not able to redefine himself and his life, and is unable to establish close relationships with other people because afraid of another loss, then that person must go backward and elaborate the meaning of the initial loss. If a woman has been victim of retaliation at work during her past years, and is now suffering of a stress during work conflicts, then she must re-elaborate the past experience and *relocate it inside a spiritual meaning*. The bilateral search, from counselor plus client, is focused in creating a continuity past-present-future, a personal identity and a meaningful connection violated-person/powerful-person. In other words, the man or the woman who have suffered from wrongs in their past shall accept the fact that also in that case they were powerful, and chose not to act because aiming to protect their own existence. At the same time, a client itself shall start to consider how innovative can be to recover painful past deeds into skills for present and future achievements. Spirituality, would thus function as a superglue interconnecting chops of wanted and undesired life events into a whole and meaningful life. To this process we can attribute the label of "*Connecting*".

In this last case, a counselor aims to relocate a client inside a whole and spiritual life. It would be thus, less appropriate for anyone to star a spiritual growth today without feeling meaningfully identified also with the own past, although painful, violent, and dreadful. In fact, the aim of a spiritual and religious growth is to integrate past negative experiences and to give them a proper value in order to see how they can be recalled as viable for a spiritual and integrated experience. Practically, a client, undergoing spiritual counseling is asked to discover how past and negative experiences can be transformed in a way for personal growth and understanding. To this process we can attribute the name of "*Rediscovering*".

Saying "Mom was bad with me" leads nowhere. While, understanding that the little girl learned to be kind to others because her mother was bad with her, is a valuable spiritual understanding and helps the subject to create a *whole spiritual self*. Even the most brilliant and altruistic persons had painful past experiences that were a milestone for their growth and identity. It is only when past sufferings are fully accepted and not elaborated, that feelings of revenge and melancholy intervene. Practically, a spiritual person might have the same biography of a rude person, with the difference, that the first re-elaborates negative past experiences and reacts to them in order to see how important they were. On the other hand, the antisocial person, having swollen the wrongs, is now unable to fill the missing parts of his/her identity and to attach a significant label to what happened to him or her. To the healthy part of this process we can give name of "*Reshaping*".

Finally, when we affirm that "*Forgiveness*" is a part of a spiritual growth, we also mean that this is not a total mental erasing of negative experiences in order to give the right of way only to what flourishes and is deemed extraordinary and positive. Indeed, this is contrary to a process of spiritual wholeness. For example, a spiritual person would instead say: "This bad thing happened in order to make me understand something about myself. I can use it to progress to higher levels of integrity and happiness".

1.13. SILENCE AND SPIRITUALITY

Keep a sacred silence in
your heart.
Your spirit is talking.

The achievement of silence can be hard. In fact, we find it difficult to find places of complete silence, but we also have little familiarity with this psychic and physical dimension. Usually, we are inclined to treat silence as a physical aspect and as a moment when a person is more focused on self and the own thoughts and feelings. But what counts most is that silence would promote in each of us an internal dialogue, with that part of our Self that somehow colours our perception, thoughts, emotions, and ideas. How to say it? When all is silent, then we are able to contact that important part of our inner life that acts as an internal little voice that we shall consider as our "Narrating Self". It tells us who we are, in any moment. It gives us advises and encourages us by reminding us that is always there, on our side.

Unfortunately, in order to be able to contact our Narrating Self, this important part of our inner life, we need to soothe the external interferences, the physical and psychic noises of our external world. It is for this reason that when we are unprepared at listening our Narrating Self, we feel in pieces, tired, unbalanced. The many puzzles of our identity cannot join in a "meaningful history". In fact, the function of our Narrating Self, of our inner dialogue, is to create a veiled but present psychic and spiritual compactness.

Only silence and meditation will allow us make a check-up of our psyche and spirit. This internal dialogue is a sort of reflection about what happens in our mind in any moment, a sort of "Cogito Ergo Sum" (I think, therefore, I am). It functions as the control panel of our car. If something is not working properly, then a warning light turns on.

Our narrating self, that works in and during silence and meditation, out of chaos, signals us well-being and discomfort of our spirit and psyche. Moreover, silence, by promoting this internal dialogue sews up again the gaps of our psyche where we have lost contact with our Self because of interfering "background noises" of our life, of physical chaos, of uproar from acoustic pollution and social crowding. Here, then, a landscape or a flower can be the starter for a mystic meditation, so our inner dialogue becomes clear. The magic atmosphere of an uncontaminated nature and its silence, or an archaeological site, helps us to contact the antique part of our self (what we have been since now) with the present one (what we are today). At the same time, the natural rhythms of nature facilitate our inner self to "move" in a similar pattern, reaching its natural wavelength fit to increase the strength of our Narrating Self. When we finally are able to tune our psychic and spiritual molecules in harmony with the natural rhythm of the universe, then our inner self and our spirituality fee satisfied because we met gain our natural and psychic movement.

Thus, internal and external movements. Internal and external sounds. There are many way to favour that internal flow that helps us feel "whole persons", and people with their own history, meaning, and continuity in life. However, the exercise of silence needs attention, training, and discernment. Feeling ourselves flying when everyday we experience the heaviness of our work or traffic jams, can inebriate or intoxicate us. Thus meaning and value of a dialogue with nature and universe can escape from us. Moreover, we might be frightened when we suddenly discover an unattended internal voice that says: "And now? Have you decided? What do you want to do of your life?". Many are thankful when this moment comes. However, many others turn on a radio and call a friend at the phone. The magnetism of solitude and silence is lost forever. We are not able to listen to "our selves". We have lost the right training. Not everyone is a champion in introspection. Instead of being carried by this beneficial internal spinning like the Derviscian whirling dancers, we reconstruct a noisy environment also in uncontaminated resorts. However if we train for silence, we will experience the space out of space, the time out of time. At this point, even a wild shore with echoes of tides braking on the shore-line can become a the starter of a dizzy and internal sound where our spirit jumps in our heart like a baby jerks into mother's womb at hearing her voice.

2

Spiritual counseling in palliative care

✦

2.1. FACILITATING MEANINGS

A spiritual quest
is a search for hidden meanings.

Many health operators, physicians, psychologists, social assistants and helpers, somewhere, in their profession, will be involved in offering psychological assistance to patients with severe illnesses. These persons could also be close friends, or even relatives or parents. For this reason, it is important to know the emotional reactions, and how values and insight change in people coping with pain and facing a disease. At the same time, there is a direct and complete involvement of the helper in these dynamics to the point that s/he often becomes a preferential interpret and a *carrier of alternative values and a facilitator for a patient's search of meanings*. In addition, spirituality has ultimately entered in workshops and journal articles as a professional instrument for the assistance of people facing terminal diseases. The same applies to spiritual counseling that, in many journals or task forces, receives guidelines and attention. This is also true in Europe for the *Royal College of Psychiatrists* in London that has created a working group in spirituality and mental health. It produces periodical workshops, articles, and a newsletter. In a recent article titled "The impact of spirituality on mental health" (Mental Health Foundation, 2006), it is suggested that the following points characterize spirituality:[39]

i)   Having the sense of a goal in life.

ii) Sense of connectedness to self, nature, Lord, and others.

iii) The search of wholeness.

iv) A search for hope and harmony.

v)   Believing in a supernatural being or entities.

vi) A certain level of transcendence, and the sense that there is much more to live than the simple materiality.

Always in a newsletter by the Royal College, it can be read that in the health professions, "Spirituality is the deep experience that one's own life has a meaning and goal together with feeling a sense of belonging" (Royal College of Psychiatrist, 2006).[40]

This description crosses transversally several religions and is placed as a common denominator for people of different religious creeds. Moreover, spirituality represents a dimension that shapes people's experiences (intra-, inter-, and transpersonal) in the communities where they live (Mental Health Foundation, 2006).[41]

Our culture, that has become much more sensitive to subjective experiences and to cultural implications of spirituality, shall be aware that this subjective dimension is a valued focal point throughout the life of a person, especially if sick or in advanced stages of a terminal disease. However, a practical implication is that also health operators and helpers, while working with terminal patients, should be equipped with personal and theoretical instruments to face, with professionalism and ease, spiritual matters of their clients. At the same time, helpers and health operators themselves should be holders of spiritual values or existential philosophies that can assist them in their existential hurdles during face-to-face contacts with patients. Conversely, in a report that evaluated the implication of nurses in the topic of spirituality, the following were emerging:[42]

- There was a lack in clarity about the concept of spirituality.

- Spiritual care was interpreted as attention to religious needs of the client.

- Spirituality is not part of the curriculum studiorum before and after nursing training.

- There was no clear vision about who should be responsible for this area.

Consequently, the peculiar condition of people with severe diseases makes the topic of spiritual counseling particularly urgent, because, perhaps for the first time, clients face issues linked to the sense of life and spirituality. In other occasions, like in conditions of poverty, needs, immigration, spirituality becomes the golden rule to start projects for the total assistance to a person. Mel Thompson in the introduction to her book, states: "People long to make sense of life; to find some key that will unlock its mysteries and enable them to understand themselves and their places within the universe. Faced with their own fragility and death, they seek courage or comfort. [...] In this human quest for meaning [...] the majority of humankind take to some form of religion".[43]

A vantage of the helper operating in a modern context is given by the existence of a historical and cultural heritage developed by the leading religious and mystical figures of our nations. They gave us important insights and writings about spirituality and human anthropology. This has partly influenced the Western and Eastern culture for palliative care to the point that many helpers match spirituality to the theme of caring, and the helping relation to *compassionate loving*. Consequently, even if a discourse on spirituality needs further investigation, a modern health operator can take advantage of many sources to reinforce his comprehension of spirituality and the anthropology of human beings: the writings of Western and Eastern religions and Mystical figures, and the literature about the *compassionate loving* in the helping relation.[44]

What seems influencing spiritual counseling with patients with severe diseases, is that both the client and his/her counselor, each time a therapeutic section begins, will start a guided and combined approach for the search of (alternative) meanings, the discovery of spiritual implications, and the understanding of a new human and existential anthropology. This is to say that, more or less "together", they will seek new ideals and goals that "transcend the common values and interpretations of life as a biological matter, at the moment threatened by a pathology".

In this reciprocal attempt to reach a shared view of what values are peculiar and important for facing loss and bereavement, I cite the Encyclical Letter of Pope John Paul the II, *Evangelium Vitae*, also because there are important ethical implications during the interactions between health operators and patients. This is particularly true if a client has lost the hope for life, is overwhelmed by pain, and is asking for euthanasia. In the Encyclical Letter *Evangelium Vitae* we can read that: "There are conditions of particular poverty, anguish, and exasperation, where the effort for survival and the pain at the limit of tolerance make the choices for the defense and promotion of life demanding, sometimes to the limit of heroism".

The particular and peculiar proximity (physical and psychological) of helpers and nurses to a patient, makes their relations and positions a privileged point for intimacy and sharing with suffering clients. This way, they assume a role of confidentiality and privileged listeners of client's quest for meaning, spiritual development, and existential search.

Ponzalo Herranz, by reporting the comments of Saint Josemarìa Escrivá de Balaguer in a letter to physicians, nurses and patients, emphasizes the closeness of the nurse (we shall add also of the helper) to the sick person. Saint Escrivà reminds to nurses: "Your work is a sacred ministry, similar to that of physicians. And even more [...] because you have the gentleness, the *immediacy*, because your are constantly close to a patient".[45] This way, we can understand why the helper, the nurse, and the responsible for palliative care, closely working with severe/terminal patients have the privilege to be the listeners and the carriers of values on life and spirituality that shall be shared and used during the helping relation. Besides, spirituality is a common experience for patients in hospital, but it is also a strategy that can enhance the assistance of health operators and their efficacy and efficiency. In fact, according to Prof. Harold Koenig, there are 5 reasons for concentrating on spirituality in patients, and are:[46]

1. "Religious beliefs and spiritual needs are common among medical patients and serve a distinct function".
2. "Religious beliefs influence medical decision making".
3. "There is a relationship between religion and both mental and physical health".
4. "Many patients would like their doctors to address these issues".
5. "There is a historical precedent for doing so".

2.2. THE STAGE OF RECEPTION

Being spiritual
means accepting
other human beings.

Anytime a person is worried about his/her own health, a cascade of emotional, social, and philosophical factors will influence basic reactions and resilience to the own diseases and to their consequences. No matter how severe this pathology can be, illness behavior has both a psychological and an existential response. The two are, then, linked to a search of meaning and to a quest for a collection of answers to what is actually occurring to the self. Practically, it is in these central moments or shortly before or after a diagnosis, that counselor's intervention will take place. Besides, the scenario in hospital just changes from an ambulatory to a ward, and from a call center to a waiting room. Moreover, a hospital is a system of interacting locations where counselor's help becomes strategic: ambulatory for diagnosis, reception, day-hospital, emergency, ward, but also waiting rooms, and call centers. Basically, if health is a primary concern in each human being, then preoccupations about health are the most threatening for patient's perception of safety, self-esteem, and resilience. Therefore, the acknowledgment a shocking and unpleasant diagnosis can be equally demanding as accommodating to positive test results after long diagnostic procedures and therapies. Moreover, hospitalization is so detrimental that a physiological stress and depression are normally found. It is, thus, a counselor's task to attend a client in order to increase his/her personal sense of self-sufficiency, well-being, satisfaction with health procedures, and compliance with diagnostic and therapeutic procedures. In general, a chain of micro-shocks and micro-stresses are daily faced by stable clients of health structures. A primary consequence is that patient's perception of safety, and counselor's clear discernment inside patient's basic needs, can be jeopardized by a condition of multiple and sequential emergencies and vital treatments onto the patient itself. At this point, in a patient, the search for meanings becomes prevalent and exclusive to the point that by leaving a client without support, a chronic and *Irreversible Hospital Emotional Shock* (IHES) can ensue. In effect, even if health events close successfully, in many people IHES can be found in their recalls of health contacts dating in the past.

Perhaps, some innocent health procedures adopted in handling that person was not sensitive to his/her emotional needs at that moment: for example, a health operator being not sensitive about some basic requests of that client. These health accidents or micro-traumas can be found in people who come back again to hospitals for further check-ups. At this time, a counselor will meet a person who is a sort of template of two emotional scripts:

- A former hospital contact with the "client A" being unattended in his/her emotional needs, this provoking an initial Hospital Emotional Shock.

- An actual hospital contact with the same "client A", this time being less resilient to health procedures because of some past micro-traumatic experience when taken in charge in hospital and another health system.

- A future hospital contact with "client A" whose reactions to further health interventions will be influenced by actual counseling strategies adopted during recent health contacts.

When a spiritual/health counselor is assigned to a patient, s/he shall face each of these parts. Therefore, a counselor shall work on patient's past emotional stresses, by helping him/her during the actual hospitalization, and by reinforcing his/her resilience by using productive counseling strategies. It is, thus, up to counselor's skill to decrease the occurrence of irreversible emotional losses and the incidence of IHES. Besides, as a constant thread in the emotional history of health clients, in any patient presenting to a hospital there is an effort to give a sense to multiple health procedures where s/he is at the center, mainly during diagnosis and treatment. Practically, a counselor becomes a preferential intermediary between health system and clients, and between clients' needs and clients' satisfactions, stress and calmness. Central to the helping relation becomes counselors' training to cope with the own personal involvement, and his/her aptitude to empathy by "acting the clients' role". Generally, only by taking on the role of clients, counselors can avoid the own phobic adjustments to health stresses by using shields or shelters of the kind "It (disease) will never get me". Consequently, the counseling of health clients requires a true and active participation of counselor to clients' life to the point that counselors themselves should be counseled to elaborate personal losses and professional stresses. This active participation, together with sincere and courageous efforts to take on a client role will open, to counselors, the multifaceted and inner experiences of their own patients. In short, by role-playing, and by playing the part of clients, health operators can familiarize and elaborate emotions –those of clients– that are scaring when unattended, although fully tolerable when elaborated inside a counseling setting. This back-and-forth process of helping and being helped, and understanding by being understood, helps counselors in mastering psychological and existential issues belonging to health clients, and to increase their own skills by reinforcing strategies of self-care and insight. In Chinese tradition there is a cultivation of the 'heart-mind' (*xin*) indicated by Mencius as the development of "compassion, shame, modesty and the distinction between right and wrong, [...] they allow the co-humanity and other virtues of a person to ripen".[47]

2.3. FROM PROFESSIONAL RECEPTION TO HUMAN WELCOMING

In spirituality
there is no higher joy
than being welcomed
by an unknown person.

The stages of taking in charge a person who has a severe/terminal disease, require a specific professional training of counselors that shall be completed also by a continuous learning on existential and spiritual subjects. This because a patient with a severe or advanced illness, approaches health operators, nurses, doctors, and helpers with "challenging" questions, or simply raises complicated existential matters. Many times, we find patients' attempts to "reorder life" and to make the last days of their own life acceptable, as if these were the milestones for their own personal well-being. In this chapter, we will meet the steps that progress from diagnosis, to the first welcoming, until the terminal care when a client is tied to bed. Besides, the task of the caretaker in assisting a client during the discovery of meanings cannot be left midway, because it is the *helper the person who mostly stays aside the clients and for longer time.*

Therefore, during the welcoming stage, apart the most popular and standard ways of "personally" supporting clients, we shall also consider more professionalized counseling strategies aiming to reduce the risk of imminent, increased, or untreatable crises in patients. In the following lines, we might visualize some common scenarios and topics belonging to the counseling of unhealthy clients.

- *"Don't worry about it, otherwise you worsen your condition".–* It could be natural for a helper the attempt to sedate a very worried person. Then, a helper, when finding out that there is nothing that can relieve a suffering patient, could be pushed "To make less dramatic" what happens, using disengagement formulas such as, "Don't worry about it, otherwise the situation worsens!". However, this approach has not, to the practical act, any effect on the anguish of a patient because it blocks the elaboration of mourning. Besides, in hospital, it is easy to meet patients who, after wrong counselors' interventions of "block of emotions", become wrapped in paper in the manifestation of their fears. In fact, they are afraid that, if they were left free to display their anguish, then their illness could even worsen. Probably, some health operator had used the "formulas of disengagement" of here above.

- *The welcome phase and the mirror experience.–* What matters most to start with the right foot is the modality with which an illness is diagnosed for the first time: if in an empathic way or a business way. Also during the next medical visits, a patient will not have to be left alone in hospital since s/he will be degraded when meeting people, in the waiting rooms, with his/her same illness but in more advanced stages.

- *"There is a person with my same illness who has recovered with alternative therapies".* – It is crucial to critically verify these affirmations of the customer who could induce him/her to cling aggressively to false hopes.

- *"I have some very strong emotions because of the therapy"*.- Usually, a therapy always represents a constant memory for a patient of his irreversible condition. That is intensified by the regular expiries when drugs are given out, (daily, weekly, etc.) or the physical therapy (e.g., chemotherapy) is scheduled. Every tablet that a patient swallows reminds him/her: "You have this disease!". It is quite useful reassuring him/her that a few effects of the therapy are, instead, attributable to his/her emotional reactions.

- *"I become stressed for each enlarged lymphonode!"*.- A hypochondriac worry, and a constant monitoring of the body, do not lack in those who suffer of a severe pathology. That, associated to anguish, could intensify little signals of the body confused as true and real symptoms of progression of a pathology: headache, several intestinal irritations, dizziness, and other.

- *Silence and solitude.*- Solitude and silence intensify the "bad thoughts" that every patient has: that is, the attention always centered on the progression of his/her illness and its consequences. Therefore, a helper can also accept a *company* function, that is, becoming a friendly presence to reduce clients' feelings of isolation.

- *"I want to solve my problems alone"*.- On the contrary, here, a patient is afraid to become a disadvantaged person, also during his elementary activities. Instead, it is suitable to stay near him/her friendly, without pestering him/her with "attitudes" that limit its autonomy.

- *"I was expecting it!"*.- A worrying pathology that is diagnosed in a sudden and unforeseeable style can produce this affirmation in a patient. By evaluating each case, a helper can accept this thought as a manifestation of patients' attempt to struggle against the idea of being in the complete hands of the fate.

- *The importance or less of a religious faith.*- Some consider their illness as a punishment rained from the sky for their faults. Instead, spiritual counseling also restores in patients the dignity and the feeling to have a value and a role in the world.

- *"The problem is that I feel well"*.- Many patients, after a while, find out that having an incurable illness not always involves supporting an intractable pain or being limited in daily activities. It is, thus, essential to explain to them than that is not exceptional.

2.4. COUNSELING IN PALLIATIVE CARE

When everything seems lost forever,
spirituality stands as a fortress
for reconstruction.

Any intervention of counseling for patients with serious/terminal illnesses stands on the following recommendation, apart from the coordination of several units and specialist figures. Practically, in order to create a supportive intervention to seriously ill patients presenting to hospital, each department has to assure a coordinated intervention of doctors, nurses, health operators, volunteers, and other helpers who talk to the same patient. This will avoid delivering to him/her contradictory messages about his/her health conditions. In fact, when a patient receives a simple piece of information seeming slightly different from those received from another health operator, s/he might develop a preoccupying crisis. From here, the need of *informing a patient with similar and coordinated messages.* In addition, it is important to create a basis for a theoretical and practical *liaison* approach between psychology and spiritual support. In other words, a patient with a severe pathology is a bearer of a double need: a *medical need* that is satisfied by the interventions on his body, and a contemporary *psycho-spiritual need* that concerns the search for a spiritual meaning in the own personal events. On the other hand, for a counselor, who is acting in hospital, a spiritual training "also" is required besides the psychological one, in order to help him/her to cure, in a total way, patients with severe and terminal illnesses. In fact, each patient turns important existential questions to a helper, and raises themes bound to spirituality and the search of a meaning in life. For example, questions like ," Why me?", "Why now?", "Why I must die?", "Why the Lord has abandoned me?", cannot be met with unplanned answers or replies simply born from "a good heart" or from "a good sense" of the health operator, and of the helper that try to meet these quests.

Finally, the creation of a team specifically trained to counsel terminal patients, foresees a multidisciplinary coordination. Here, doctors, nurses, and other health operators jointly work together with clergymen. Everyone, with no distinction, is specifically trained it in the field of the existential problems during death and dying. However, what counts more is that nurses, helpers and clergymen are interdependent and not "wrapped" each one in its own duty without the possibility of assuming one the role of the other. Indeed, a helper will have to be responsible "also" for the existential and the theological aspects of death and dying. On the other hand, a minister shall be ready to offer also a psychological assistance to the illness in the department where s/he works in. Therefore, the creation of a practical tool is necessary. In a word, a psycho-spiritual therapy is easily applicable by every health operator and helper working in hospital. Besides, psycho-spiritual counseling, shall consider specific training moments, born from a mingling of experiences on the field, (example, the counseling "Bed Side" to the bed patients), and from theoretical lessons on existentialism and theology. Basically, the team adopting a spiritual counseling will have to strive to be homogeneous in its answers and its techniques of reception of patients, by using spiritual counseling, communication, and interpersonal skills equally shared amongst the member of the team. In fact, here, there is not a doctor who is occupied "only for" or a nurse responsible "only for".

2.5. A MULTIFACETED PROBLEM

> *When I get no answers from life,*
> *my soul pours fresh ideas*
> *into the emptiness of the*
> *scaring unknown.*

A person with a serious and final illness can present a pain bound not only to the mourning event or the hopelessness, but also to the sense or meaning of this loss in his/her own existence. This sense is usually interpreted and reinterpreted according to two core quests:

- Existential research: how a patients "philosophically" reconsiders his/her life by searching/researching for a new "sense" when comparing what s/he is today with what s/he was yesterday, before of the crisis.

- Spiritual research: how a patient interprets/reinterprets "spiritually" its own existence by looking for answers from his/her creed that might give a sense to the Self as an entity gifted with faith towards a God and towards religion.

If an illness, daily events, hospital experiences, and daily occupations find no placement inside a sense or meaning, then a patient could have a pain that not only is psychological, emotional, affective, but also spiritual and moral. For this reason, spiritual counseling helps the patients during their search for a meaning to be attributed to their own psychic and physical pain. In addition, the efforts to reach a peaceful explanation are often preceded by a series of questions and assertions that are subdivisible in existential, spiritual, and psychological:

- *Existential requests:*
1. "Why me?".
2. "Why must I die?".
3. "What sense has life, my life?".
4. "Why is all this happening to (me)?".
5. "I have done so much in my life. What has it served to?".
6. "What will be of me and my family after me?".

- *Doubts and assertions of spiritual kind:*
7. "Why has the Lord not listened to my prayers?".
8. "Why has the Lord abandoned me?".
9. "Does God really exist?".
10. "I have done all good in my life and the Lord has punished me".
11. "What happens after death?".
12. "Why does the Lord not take me with him soon?".
13. "Does the Lord want to tell me something?".
14. "My faith has got stronger".

- *Affirmations and psychological themes:*
15. "And if the others noticed?".
16. "I make strong efforts to keep a certain quiet façade".
17. "I want to make the others aware of my illness!". "In the moments of anger I would like to blab everything!".
18. "I fear that the news can scatter!".
19. "One can never be pure. I am afraid that people mumble".
20. "Not knowing it would have been better".
21. "My mind wonders around".
22. "There is a doctor who uses a different therapy".
23. "The alternative therapies do not hurt as much as those they administer in hospital".

24. "And if I were not able to recover any more?".

25. "What does it change by knowing that I am sick?".

Thus, we can consider spiritual counseling in hospital also like a way of living the relationship with patients, which means a way to answer to the encounter that completes and extends an empathic cordial, human, and charitable approach. In other words, spiritual counseling becomes a place, and an intervention where two people cross the boundaries of the self and the spirit in a mutual approach and relief, to discuss about profound issues about life, pain, disease, death, and dying. That wants to mean that what really matters is the "relationship" doctor/ health operator-patient, which moves, draws, and is based on existential and spiritual assumptions. This requires a certain anthropological vision of human sufferings. Any patient during the last moments of the own existence, strives not to lose his or her own *humanities*. S/he does not escape any more from the sensitivity and the biological pain. On the contrary, s/he does of this event, the moment of maximum communion with the self and the world.

Therefore, behind the human being who suffers, there is also a person who notices the Self. S/he is a person whose introspection becomes deeper and deeper as the illness progresses, and the own destiny becomes a constant concern. In this journey, that is also spiritual, a patient will make the helper come in his/her "private psychic circle", mutually sharing all personal torments but also the own spiritual understanding. Nevertheless, this internal circle of any patient can also be a place for an anonymous agony and an untouchable pilgrimage of the spiritual soul where the helper can enter only if invited. Everything depends on then empathy and on the spiritual training of this counselor.

Besides, a spiritual journey can be healing for patients as long as their personal tragedy and affliction are viable of spiritual explanation, which means, in patients' mind, being able to attribute a *human, spiritual, existential, and psychic meaning*. A spiritual counselor, in order to be invited and to be able to counsel afflicted clients, shall be, thus, ready to share this spiritual journey and stand, together with clients, the burden of suffering, pain, and sorrow. On the other hand, a helper, as a Good Samaritan, becomes, for a patient, an instrument for emotional resonance, a meaning creator, and a spiritual transformer of the "seemingly senseless happenings" in client's life and comments. At the same time, a spiritual counselor, would interpret what happens in the here-and-now dyadic exchange with clients, and would filters the own emotional and spiritual dynamic experience in order to reflect new insights to clients. Without this courage, by part of helpers, to fully embrace clients' existential and spiritual turmoil, spiritual counseling would be deprived of one of its core instruments.

2.6. TALKING ABOUT THE MEANING OF LIFE

Nothing else, apart from spirit,
stands alive
when the leaves fall
and the forces fade away.

"The meaning of life" is a concept that introduces us to the existential/experiential basis of the interaction between helpers and ill persons. It focuses mainly on the sense that the ill person is searching in his/her own life, now endangered by the existence of a serious/terminal disease. Consequently, some peculiar spiritual contents appear as recurrent during spiritual/health conversation between health operators and patients:

1. What is the actual meaning of life, especially when following the diagnosis of a preoccupying illness?
2. What is the meaning of death and dying?
3. What family and close relationships will develop during disease, death, and dying (the 3 "D")?
4. The own destiny after death, and the empty space left in the own role and duty in society: e.g. a patient is an important manager, or s/he is the principal force in the own family, etc.
5. The life of its darlings after patient's death and the anguish to leave, behind, some undefended survivors.
6. His/her own soul, that is, patient's own spiritual dimension, and what is waiting him/her after death according to the own religious creed.
7. The conclusion of the own existence, and the effort to give a meaning to what apparently and culturally seems a private deed, emptied of every value.

Besides, a spiritual counselor is a companion in the pilgrimage of an ill person to the point that all existential meanings will be part and participant of all the interactions with his/her patient. In addition, this is a dynamic approach because the construction of spiritual meanings rises and develops according to the characteristics of the relationship between counselors and patients. There is, thus, no standard intervention in this approach or confirmed theories. Basically, the dynamics of this kind of approach is demanding for both clients and helpers. In fact, each value shall be tailored according to people, social and psychological situation, stage of illness, and community resources available (churches, affiliation, membership to religious congregations), etc.

2.7. SPIRITUALITY AND HEALTH OPERATOR

Spirituality is a sort of vitamin:
it is good for everybody.

Spiritual counseling emphasizes the interpersonal relationship as a core strategy for the free flow (often bilateral) of spiritual meanings between counselors and clients. Without the existence of a solid and resistant strategy as a guide to the content of this interaction, a spiritual counselor cannot proceed efficiently in the relationship. In addition, s/he has to keep in mind that there is some line of reasoning that characterizes this approach.

1. Unlike a normal psychotherapeutic setting, during spiritual counseling there cannot be any application of the term "pathology".

2. A spiritual counselor must familiarize with the whole range of emotional reactions of a person facing death and dying.

3. A spiritual counselor has relatively a short time to arrange a traditional counseling setting. Here, a counselor must indeed rely upon few months, few weeks, or even few days in order to reach a satisfying relationship with patients and to implement a spiritual approach. Nonetheless, this minor door can be enough in order to start a spiritual counseling and to select the most cogent topics on religion, spirituality, and life that are the actual concerns for a patient.

4. A patient might ask to be helped in reaching a higher understanding of his/her personal event, a higher *insight*, a more profound faith, a brighter perception of all spiritual anchorages.

5. During spiritual counseling, there is an increased risk of a preoccupying burnout in counselors and helpers just because of the topics treated. For this reason, it is mandatory a personal training on issues related to death and dying, palliative care, etc.

What comes first is that each spiritual counselor shall have undertaken a specific training on self-help about these topics. This means that s/he should have already elaborated the own "*philosophy on life and spirituality*". *In fact, at the basis of spiritual counseling, there is the idea that counselors can help clients if they are able to help themselves whenever they feel the dread of being in the place of their patients. In other words, spiritual counselors shall be able to spiritually rescue themselves when they imagine to be "at the place of" a client, of a seriously ill patient, of a needy person, of a discouraged poor person, etc.* Therefore, in order to achieve this important condition of *identification* with terminal patients, helpers shall go through a specific experiential/personal training in the *as-if* conditions, trying to elaborate spiritual strategies when imagining to being at the place of their patients in specific painful circumstances. Besides, through guided role-playing, the trainees in spiritual counseling shall be helped to use mature and practical spiritual coping strategies whenever immerged in the palliative care theatre: pre-test and post-test counseling, hospitalization, worsening of health, dying in clear consciousness. Therefore, during the core stages of a serious illness, each counselor shall be prompted to find coping strategies (spiritual and psychological) to be applied to real clients. Indeed, any phobic reaction to escape from the role-play shall be interpreted and elaborated for learning. However, also trainees' mature responses will be reinforced because they will probably be used during real interactions with real clients. As a conclusion, during training in spiritual counseling, *the higher the dexterity in identification with clients in the as-if conditions, the higher the chance to personally elaborate exhaustive responses for the self and the others, and the higher the likelihood to be successful in spiritual help of terminal patients.*

Usually, spiritual counseling, addressed to serious and terminal patients, has as a founding basis in the direct relationship between a helper and its client. Practically, spiritual counseling is a sort of vibrant dance of emotions, meanings, misunderstandings, fears, anxieties, discoveries, and satisfactions on both sides of the dyad: patient and counselor. Nevertheless, it is mainly an open and genuine dialogue on the cogent themes of existence, life, death, dying, God, etc. Here, meanings are created and re-created in a dynamic movement towards client's higher well-being.

From here, we are able to select the features of a spiritual approach for what concerns the format of the relationship between counselors and their patients:

1. *Sympathy,* as complementary to empathy, meaning a personal genuine involvement of the counselor, who emotionally embraces the event, and who is able to catch the core spiritual questions of clients. These last might not be able to translate their personal sufferings into a spiritual quest yet.

2. *Empathy*, usually meant as the counselor's ability to being in the shoes of patients, but namely, and here, also as the strategy to predict the whole development of patient's event and to foresee spiritual strategies to limit his/her future losses of hope.

3. *Non-verbal spiritual communication* is the ability to continue spiritual counseling also with patients that are loosing contact with reality, are inside an irreversible muteness, or are unable to move or talk. Here, too, a counselor shall be capable of transforming this intense moment of sharing into an act of shared spiritual meanings and growth.

4. *A diagnostic framing of the counseling relationship* means that a spiritual counselor makes any effort in abandoning psychopathological categories. Instead, s/he sees any "suffering man and woman" as a unique being, in a stage of "physical minus" but as an enthusiastic person who is starting a singular pilgrimage inside the own personal growth. Here, the client/patient asks to the helper a whole involvement and a full participation in the personal quest for meaning.

Finally, we shall interpret the spiritual counseling, as spirituality *in the approach*. In other words a "peculiar way" of any counselor to face the lacks of meanings when present in patients, and a readiness to talk about life and death as any spiritually oriented person would do. This spiritual *savoir-faire* partly responds to the ethics of spiritual relationships and encompasses a way of interacting by disclosing emotions and identities, much more than communicating words. This affectionate encounter naturally develops from its initial premises: a mutual respect and a reciprocal understanding of the personhood present in the other fellow.

2.8. TARGET AND COUNSELING STAGES

A relief for every kind of pain
is being reassured in the spirit.

Spiritual counseling of the critical and terminal patient differentiates amongst several stages of the assistance according to the stage of development of the illness and the point of recovery. Other distinctions are made on the basis of the progression of a pathology, the severity of pain and if tolerable, the awareness of being ill/very ill, the existence of an emotional support from family or community, the exigency of an economic assistance, or the degree of spiritual maturity and religious involvement. Following, there is a short list of the spiritual and medical history that spiritual counselors need to know about resources and gaps in the conscience of their clients. Other aspects will be examined more in detail.

1. *Stage of illness in a patient.*– It represents the first indicator of the style of a contemplated intervention. In fact, the emotional state that accompanies a recent notification of a terminal illness will be different from that of the terminal stages of the same illness, when the organic debilitation and the emotional stress are already in a chronic phase.

2. *Pain is bearable.*– Patients affected by serious and terminal illnesses always question themselves about possible painful consequences of their own clinical condition, the "supportability" of their pain, and side effects of a therapy. Aside from the availability of analgesic medicines, a serious and terminal patient must be helped to face themes about "pain" with clear information, with proposals of hope, and with a psychological support focused not so much on their "disease" but much on "pain".

3. *The typologies of "pain".*– They represent the worries of serious and terminal patients, and can be divided in the following categories:

- *The Psychic Pain.*– As consequence of the discovery of an illness.

- *The Social Pain.*– From the thoughts about family affections and about the "vacant place" that will be created after patient's own death ("Who will deal with my family?").

- *The Occupational Pain.*– Uncertainties about the possibility to succeed in continuing his/her own job, and to finish what has been dormant ("Who will take care of my business?").

- *The Biographical Pain.*– Tied to events or facts that are undeveloped in his/her own life, and that require a decisive intervention ("I would like to reconcile myself with my brother!").

- *The Information Pain.*– It means that a patient regrets not to have tried enough in "better" clinical centers or feeling deprived of "better therapies".

- *The Waiting List Pain.*– A patient suffers from the incapability to get in rapid and serene ways interventions of diagnosis and therapy, for example, s/he is unable to move of region or nation to get a CAT scan or a magnetic resonance.

- *The Pain of the Abandoned Patient.*– It refers to the patient's awareness of his/her own poverty and of being a client of third category that cannot receive the essential therapies for his/her own illness.

- *The Pain of the "Field Hospital".*– It refers to conflicting relationships between a patient and physicians or nurses because of ways "not totally" human and polite of these in managing a patient's own suffering and his/her own fears: "Feeling a simple number" ("They treat me as a shoe!").

- *Spiritual Pain.*– A patient sees his/her own illness as "guilt" to expiate; s/he thinks that the own illness represents a moment of "abandonment"; s/he nourishes doubts about the "mercy" of the Lord; s/he suspects of the "divine goodness", etc.

Pain can be, thus, revealed by several emotions, expressed through a variety of feelings, and all synonyms of the emotional suffering experienced by a patient:

- Disappointment
- Regret
- Hopelessness
- Chagrin
- Exasperation
- Failure
- Shame
- Angst
- Panic
- Anxiety

As it regards the categories on which counseling can intervene we remember:

1. *"Undeveloped circumstances".*– They can be considered "open gestalts" where a client is helped to close, conclude, and end whatever stays open, dormant, unattended, etc.

2. *"Indefinite situations"*.– In this case, it could be suitable a cognitive intervention aiming to deliver information and to outline every single worry and fear that a patient is experiencing.

3. *"Emotional situations"*.– In this case, an existential approach or counseling can help a patient to contain the blandest situations.

4. *Situations of serious anxiety, phobia and panic attacks*.– We can think about an approach aiming to deliver information and to techniques of exposure in imagination: for example, fear to become "deformed" because of the therapies. A lot of cognitive-behavioral techniques allow an exposure in fantasy to feared situations that usually represent a process of "catastrophic thoughts" intensified by the fears of clients on the less known aspects of their own illness.

5. *Situations of mild depression*.– We need interpersonal therapy for depression leading a client to intensify the bonds with "pleasant" and friendly social groups. In addition, meetings of group therapy for patients in the same stage of illness can serve to such a purpose. The instillation of hope from a group of peers, better if formed by those people who have already overcome the initial stages of an illness, is more powerful than every reassurance from an outsider, even if it comes from a counselor. At the same time, the participation to religious ceremonies and spiritual meetings can reinforce strategies to overcome depression. What counts most is that a patient receives from other church attendees the permission to contact them, and to phone them when feeling down or overwhelmed by catastrophic thoughts about the own illness.

6. *Situations of serious and uncontrollable anxiety*.– Some anti-anxiety drugs can be proposed. Also sections of expressive therapy based on religious topics can be helpful.

7. *Situations of serious insomnia and chronic difficulty to sleep*. – Exercises of relaxation or informative counseling can be used to reassure those, many in reality, that are afraid to sleep because worried about "dying when sleeping".

8. *Writing a diary and the own autobiography*.– Besides favoring the process of the creation of a sense, this allows to a client "to observe himself/herself from the outside". This shall help him/her to find a moment of relief from a story (the own illness) lived, for its own nature, completely from the inside.

2.9. CAN SPIRITUALITY HOLD PLACEBO EFFECTS?

Nothing comes unexpected
in the miracles
produced by spiritual medicine.

Can we attribute some of the healing effects of a spiritual approach to patients' expectations and hope? Some interesting finding in this direction can be found in the theories of placebo. The word "placebo" from Latin future tense "I will please", in medicine is used to denominate an inert preparation (usually, containing sugar, lactose, amid, sugared water or olive oil) with no therapeutic effect. It works only if s/he who takes the placebo is convinced of assuming a real drug. However, even though the word "placebo" belongs to modern medicine, man has always been influenced by placebo and placebo effects in the traditional care and self-healing. The cures proposed by Shamans and "Curanderos", utilizing "curative powders, dried insects or organic specimens" is a form of placebo therapy. What is important is that who takes them is convinced about the medicine and the curative power of the healer. Professors Shapiro A. K. and Shapiro E., state that the placebo effect is that produced by official drugs at sub-therapeutic doses.[48] Now the placebo effect, the classical "sugar pill", is used with a therapeutic aim to relief anxiety, headache, post-surgical pain, asthma crises, depression and high blood pressure. Prof. Hróbjartsson (in the *European Journal Clinical Pharmacology*), holds 3 main explanations for the placebo effect: 1) the "opioid model" where the placebo evokes the release from brain, of endorphins; 2) the "conditioning model" where patients respond with healing because they have learned to do so as automatic mechanism when dealing with doctors or hospitals; 3) the "meaning or expectancy model" where patient's expectations about positive outcomes about care and therapy initiates self-healing processes.[49] These studies underpin again the power of body-mind connection, and the fact that when mind believes that it is receiving a cure, then it starts a beneficial effect on body and a process of self-healing. However, the placebo effect, alias the process of self-healing and patients' expectation, also play a central role in spiritual counseling, but also in any psychotherapy. According to Prof. Harold Koenig, "We know that if the patient believes in the doctor and believes in the treatment, then the treatment will be more effective. The placebo response is based on the belief of the patient in the treatment. [...] (This) may cause actual physiological changes that move the patient toward recovery".[50]

From the studies of placebo, nowadays, we have a new philosophy of healing and care, which attributes as central factor in therapy and healing, something similar to what emerged in placebo studies: patients' expectation, hope, and trust in the therapeutic relationship with doctors. Thus, suggestibility or expectation of the client, together with the acceptance of the counselor, added to the empathic and ethical approach of this last, are central in starting any healing and cure. In fact, Prof. Spiro, in his book "The Power of Hope", suggests to doctors to play particular attention to the cure based on the placebo effect, because it is focused on an empathic and considerate approach to clients.[51]

Suggestion and expectation, as Prof. Carol Hart explains, represent the favorable attitudes of patients towards doctors and therapy, and they are essentials for a fast recovery.[52] I feel that modern therapy and counseling, shall seek for the placebo effect, not only with the classical sugar-pill, but also as a therapeutic force for healing. In fact, in order to reach the full work alliance, and to start the process of patients' healing, a spiritual counselor shall obtain the full trust from patients, also presenting him/herself as a trustworthy person. Moreover, a therapist shall be optimistic about the own approach and skills, and, mainly, about client's power for self-healing. In conclusion, doctors and counselors, shall overcome, through a warm, human, empathic, and professional behavior, the barrier of incredulity and skepticism in their clients. The placebo effect, then, would rise not from the "copy pill", but, instead, from the therapist who feels personally and truly convinced about the own ability to cure and heal. Another important factor in the "placebo suggestion" is the factor trust, beyond the expectation and the hope issues. In fact, as Prof. Lasagna underlines, a central factor in the therapeutic failure and in the lack of healing is the mistrust of patients toward their own therapist.[53]

We shall then think that who obtains better therapeutic results and easier spiritual/psychological healing, namely, who better uses the "therapeutic placebo effect", (being similar the drugs and the approaches used) are therapists or hospitals that achieve higher degrees of acceptance and trust from people, patients, and clients. Instead, if a patient holds a *negative expectation*, if it is sad because in conflict with, and discouraged about physicians, therapists, hospitals, s/he will then no longer react and respond to therapy or placebo. In sum, the enchantment is broken. The body no longer responds to mind, and the pathology get worst, and it becomes harder to cure and heal that person. In this case, the placebo effect turned into the opposite, the "nocebo". It equally happens if physicians or psychologists are skeptical about their own power and skills. So that, when they propose a therapy (medical or psychological), they lack of a magic touch, seem mechanical, detached, apparently uninterested to client's opinion. By missing an empathic and professional relationship, these health operators do not evoke a favorable hope in clients and reduce their positive expectations. In fact, as the Professors Shapiro demonstrated, even official drugs and therapies delivered at sub-therapeutic does, or with limited effects on symptoms, ends by becoming miraculous, if the therapists who propose them believe that they are good and efficacious, and, at the same time, are able to establish an empathic relationship with clients.[54]

These findings show that clients' trust, hope, and positive expectation make the final goals of a "good medicine, psychotherapy, and spiritual counseling". Here, placebo effect and real therapeutic effect sum up and mix together. Moreover, a successful counselor knows how to mix a therapeutic *savoir-faire* with other basic ingredients, like suggestibility, empathy, trust, and charisma. However, those who less respond to the placebo effect are neurotic or hypochondriac subjects.[55]

From these finds, we can now draw some guidelines about the pros and cons to spiritual counseling, and the strategies to generate a therapeutic force for cure and healing:

- *The role of the counselor.–* Constant empathy, trustworthy attitudes, and warm attention towards clients are the first steps towards healing. Consequently, it becomes central the *charisma* of a spiritual counselor. Only people gifted with certain ascendancy and respectability to the eyes of the patients can generate hope and a positive expectancy. On the contrary, a cold and detached attitude cancels the enchantment and discourages the client's hope to be able to find benefit from that doctor or psychologist and the proposed therapies. The charisma of the counselor is, therefore, fundamental, together to his/her credibility, and inclination to the human relationship with patients.

- *Constant attention and focus on the follow-up of the client.–* The counselor who wants to promote cure and healing shows a constant focus to clients and follow-up. S/he follows a client in any stage, starting from the initial encounter, if a client has been assigned to him or her. As Prof. Carol Hart notices, the only attention of a respectful therapist is able to reduce client's anxiety.[56]

- *The infusion of hope.–* Every therapy has failure phases. It happens both with the traditional and official drugs, and with partial or exclusive placebo. Therefore, it is always helpful the infusion of hope in clients. In order to obtain cure and healing, a counselor shall monitor the reasons of client's mistrust and discouragement. A placebo effect and a psychic improvement do not emerge if a patient is, or feels, deserted.

- *An ethical approach.–* The suggestion can turn easily into plagiarism if used by specialists without scruples. Consequently, it is always necessary that a doctor and a psychologist have in mind such side of the human psyche. In fact, it is easy to deceive weak people and change a placebo in a false optimism, and a positive expectation into a groundless hope. In other words, the placebo effect must be seriously considered, as a true and real therapy. In fact, a slight misunderstanding about hope and illusion, wish and reality, approved therapies and unorthodox strategies, could really endanger client's physical and psychic well-being.

2.10. Talking "spiritual"

*Words from your
heart and glances
from your soul.
Nothing else is needed for
a true spiritual healing.*

Interpersonal relationships, and verbal communication in the health system, make the core strategies for delivering any medical, psychological, social, and spiritual therapy to clients and patients. Moreover, through verbal communication, important medical information is acquired and transmitted. In addition, as spiritual counseling principally focuses on a personal encounter between counselors and clients, then the style and content of what is communicated becomes the preferential strategy to promote spiritual health, growth, and faith. Besides, spiritual counseling with patients is carrier also of important information centered on profound issues about death and dying. Hence, a spiritual counselor shall become familiar with some cogent aspects of communication, spirituality, and health behavior. Specifically, we are interested in how spiritual counseling is able to influence health behaviors of any person, for example, by helping in the adherence to therapeutic regimens or medical therapies. Furthermore, it is significant to define the core styles of communication that make the difference in spiritual counseling.

Specifically, what are the interpersonal and verbal exchanges that can be labeled as "spiritual" and, what instead is counselor's behavior and attitude that is not crucial for spiritual counseling. I met very good pastors with a weak spiritual communication. On the other side, I was surprised of the high "spiritual communication" in laymen and people with a high devotion. What is then a "spiritual communication"? Practically, the questions are: "What are the styles that a counselor shall use in order to promote and improve patient's spirituality, faith, and growth?". Second: "What are the communication styles in spiritual counseling?". Whenever we shed light to peculiar aspects of spiritual encounters between counselors and patients, we become aware of how central verbal communication is in counseling and, specifically, spiritual counseling.

Practically, a counselor shall have trained verbal skills to communicate love, attention, affection, consideration, support, etc. Each one of the emotional stages of spiritual counseling regularly relies upon specific verbal statements and styles. Besides, it is the constant presence and participation of the spiritual counselor in a patient's life and disease that assures the maintenance and the reinforcement of the stages of growth achieved. Thus, any further delay in contacting a patient, or any encounter that has no embedded hints for a next meeting, would weaken a patient's growth, well-being, and spiritual achievements. Basically, spiritual counseling, as we have seen many times, is a continuous dialog between two people who become closer and closer as time passes. Yet, in order to achieve a sense of self-fulfillment and spiritual satisfaction, a patient must feel the constant reassurance and physical presence of a spiritual counselor. This approach is time demanding while spiritual counselors are practically under constant watch by part of their clients. Each word, expression, glance of a counselor is constantly monitored by clients in search of sighs of approval, or further reinforcement for the own soul or relief for their own sorrow.

Thus, counselor's verbal communication becomes the corner stone for patient's psychic and physical survival. In addition, any health behavior and the maintenance of strict therapeutic regimens in hospital reflect the quality and quantity of verbal exchanges between health operators, patients, parents, pastors, etc. Just because a patient is highly vulnerable, s/he will feel that verbal comments coming from health personnel bear the same importance of any technical and medical information. Practically, in patient's soul and mind there is no differentiation between words of encouragement, medical information, and diagnoses. In a word, whatever is "told" to patients in hospital, becomes the pivot for their well-being or desperation.

2.11. SPIRITUAL AND MEDICAL INFORMATION

In a hospital,
spiritual talk and
medical jargon
are allied to
promote patient's joy.

For a sort of natural selection, in hospital, "everything is information and everything is important". Practically, there could be no easy differentiation between what makes a spiritual communication and what makes medical or technical information. Constantly we find a high degree of patient's emotional involvement in any stage of his/her own daily events. In addition, interpersonal relationships, and verbal communication in the health system make the core strategies for delivering any medical, psychological, social, and spiritual therapy to clients and patients. Also, through verbal communication, information is acquired and transmitted. What is more, important and basic medical interventions can be assured by the right bi-directional (from and to patients) flow of "words" passing from health operators to their clients and vice versa. In this multifaceted process of interpersonal verbal exchanges between clients and health operators, basic ethics rules suggest that clients' well-being shall be achieved by equally supporting their spiritual as well their physical well-being. Moreover, the success in verbal exchanges between health operators and clients are essential for the delivery of better cures, clear diagnoses, proper therapeutic regimens and to assure clients' compliance and satisfaction.

As also seen, it is the constancy and the quality of proper verbal exchanges and emotional support of patients that practically assure their well-being, while the continuation of "satisfying" verbal exchanges would allow any recovery from diseases, or the observance of therapeutic and behavioral regimens. Nonetheless, only through a progressive transformation of a technical talk into a spiritual and emotional talk, health operators would increase their own chances to make a breach into client's sufferings, resistances, and skepticism. On the other hand, the abandonment of the client and the persistence of a "technical approach" without importing elements of emotional, spiritual, and religious support will lower patient's health behaviors and the feeling of being treated with "professionalism and love". On the whole, it is also intuitive stating that the proper training in interpersonal communication and the wise use of verbal strategies can allow the achievement of better cures by part of health operators. On patients' side, there will be an increase in personal well-being, health, and satisfaction with the medical procedures.

To summarize, the acquisition of the core strategies in verbal communication in the health system as in any other setting focused on the help of needy people, is central for the success of "any other" intervention that requires "words and verbal information" in order to proceed. It is also intuitive stating that the proper training in interpersonal communication and a wise use of verbal strategies can allow the achievement of better cures by part of health operators. Furthermore, in cases of serious illnesses, technical information is styled according to the spiritual-emotional requirements of the stressed client, and vice versa, spiritual communication carries a large amount of information about each aspect of psychological and physical health. Only by achieving the proper blend between technicalities and spiritualities in health communication, there will be an increase in client's well-being, health, and satisfaction with medical procedures. To summarize, the acquisition of the core strategies in verbal communication for an integrated spiritual-medical approach, in the health system, is central for the success of "any other" health intervention that requires "words and verbal information" in order to proceed. Moreover, the development of spiritual communication strategies in health operators, and technical communication strategies in spiritual counselors, complement any other approach to the sick person. It would be thus central to register the proper communication theories and strategies to be implemented during spiritual/medical therapy. In this last instance, we shall talk about *Spiritual/Technical Information Strategies* or, shortly, *STIS*.

2.12. THE CENTRAL ROLE OF VERBAL COMMUNICATION IN SPIRITUAL COUNSELING

Talk to the soul,
reach the spiritual mind,
and you will heal the body.

In this paragraph, we shall try to transit on some basic theories and practical strategies to implement personal and interpersonal skills in verbal communication. The setting hypothesized is that where on one side we find a specialist helper (psychologist, nurse, doctor, health worker, social worker, family doctor, etc.), on the other side, we usually meet their clients or patients. Any verbal exchange between these two people has the following goals:

- To deliver information aiming to the psychological or physical well-being of clients.

- To create a moment of interpersonal interaction to increase the psychological well-being of a client and to relieve his/her psychological or physical pain.

- To listen to what the client tells and to empathically respond to this input.

• To inform a client about medical information, diagnoses, therapies, and recovery strategies.

Much of the subsequent health behaviors adopted in debilitating or chronic diseases is very likely a matter of the earliest verbal exchanges between health operators, counselors, and their clients or patients. Besides, also rational health behaviors or actions impeding a full recovery of healthier conducts are a dynamical and emotional reaction of patients to precarious verbal exchanges, information, and interpersonal interactions with nurses, doctors, or primary caretakers. On the other hand, a tactful and spiritual manner of communicating can promote better health and well-being. This is even more significant during the pre-test and post-test periods, when a diagnosis of a disease or the announcement of a therapeutic chronic regimen is delivered to a client for the first time. Practically, any subsequent success or failure in the psychosocial and medical support of new patients heavily responds to their reactions during multiple moments where important and vital information transit from health personnel to clients and vice versa.

The challenge is to investigate better strategies for verbal-spiritual communication linked to patient's care. Besides, it is implied that although non-verbal communication still stands as a central skill during any psychosocial and medical care, verbal communication, by carrying the principal medical and technical information important for the life of patients, is also the main venue for people's health, satisfaction, and adoption of dietary/medical/therapeutic regimens in hospital. There are, thus, many ways and moments in which true information can be delivered through tactful manners yet being ineffective because some interpersonal strategies were weakly monitored, and a human approach not reinforced. In addition, the dyad informant-informed is the pivot for any health behavior and suggested therapeutic measures. Through this encounter there will be a continuous flow of verbal exchanges all carrying a blended content of medical, technical, spiritual and psychological data. At this point, the core question becomes: "How is patient's health behavior affected by the initial contacts and verbal exchanges with health operators adopting spiritual/technical communication?". Which conducts to the implied question: "Is health behavior in medicine 'also' the end result of verbal exchanges of information between primary health operators and clients adopting an integrated medical/spiritual communication style?". We know from history how "therapeutic" for health, and magnetic for personal growth, was the verbal exchange of needy people with persons holding a particular charisma. Not only are "doctors that cure" clever scientists and empathic people, but they also equally adopt verbal strategies of information that are a combined format of medical, technical, and spiritual expressions.

For example, something is telling to a patient: "You have a severe illness. Let's see what we can do". Something else is stating: "Mr. White, I will try to do all my best to find together with you a comfortable way to cope with this condition". Perhaps, both are stating the same thing, but the emotional contact and proximity between two people offered by the second example, is closer to a "spiritual" way to handle diseases and patients.

The ethical importance of the right information through verbal exchanges with patients is an intuitive understanding. In other words, the failure to self-care and well-being, whenever the right information seems being delivered, can hypothetically be attributed to some of the following:

- Information was not clear, and there was no feedback from a client prompted by the direct health operator. A client thus failed in health behaviors because adopted wrong strategies depending on the semantic complexity or confusion deriving form the verbal strategies adopted by caretakers. Here, the scheme is: *Semantic Complexity → Behavioral Stop*.

- Information was clear and simple, yet the wording used was not respecting client's understandings, emotions, and feelings at the moment. The client failed to adopt health behaviors because the interpersonal code of ethics was somehow infringed. *Semantic Simplicity vs. Behavioral Stop*

- Information was clear, the wording understandable, and the semantic content of the information was respecting the code of ethics for interpersonal exchanges in health settings. Consequently, the patient adopted health behaviors "also" as consequence of a positive reaction to the verbal strategies adopted by health operators. *Semantic Simplicity → Behavioral Modification*

- Information was semantically complex, yet the adoption of an ethical code of interpersonal relationships helped a client to seek for further explanations that were delivered in understandable manners. Health behaviors were adopted as a positive emotional response to the dynamic of the interpersonal exchanges more than as a result of the complex information. People with low education or low social class much respond this way. Their focus of attention on the "person" (quality of the nurse or doctor), and interpersonal trust is a paramount for any further adoption of therapeutic and dietary regimens. *Semantic Complexity + Spiritual talk → Behavioral Modification*.

Another strategy for delivering complex information is through the use of metaphors. Yet their use implies a wise understanding of patient's milieu and the mental complexity of clients. Religious literature is full of teachings of big thinkers delivered by using metaphorical examples. In fact, by adopting a simple but profound language, complex information can become comprehensible. Therefore, the use of pictorial images to deliver complex medical information can be suggested. At the same time, if the metaphorical information contains competent metaphorical images, religious examples, and analogous histories extracted from speeches of important religious leaders, then a doctor or a counselor have proved strategies for being clear to patients and tactful also with technical communication.

2.13. SPIRITUAL COUNSELING AND EXPRESSIVE THERAPIES

Spiritual care
is when we pour fresh water
of love onto a dry spirit.

It seems unusual to talk about expressive therapy in a book about spiritual counseling. We usually have in mind the classical approach and the "therapy through words" that frame a therapeutic encounter between any counselor and a patient. Nevertheless, in a spiritual approach to seriously ill patients, "words" can be difficult to manage, especially with patients in a critical stage, or with those who are silenced by a profound turmoil and by clear worries. I felt that when I started sections of expressive therapies with terminal patients, spirituality was there, embracing any moment of the creation of people still able to express themselves from the depth of silence and pain. The following lines are a short account about the potentials that expressive therapies can bring to spiritual counseling. Practically, I would propose to enclose expressive therapies in the frame of techniques for spiritual counseling

When I started to practice counseling for HIV positive people, in a major teaching hospital with an AIDS clinic, I believed that the traditional empathic approach could have been enough to satisfy any requirement of many young people facing the specter of terminal diseases. However, soon, I found that this method was not enough, like any other psychotherapy addressed to very sick people. Moreover, I felt that I was not able to be very helpful during long hospitalizations, or during the latest stages of an illness. Besides, patients' discomfort added to my helplessness during their terminal stages, when they were not able to have enough strength or motivation to embrace any offering in counseling and psychotherapy. In many cases, hospitalization lasted weeks or months, and often these were the last days of their life. At the same time, I was required to "do something" to bring an additional help to colleagues. Initially, the idea of using expressive therapies as complement to spiritual counseling came during some encounters with patients that brought in their rooms some papers and colors.

Gradually, I found that during the period of engagement in creative activities (painting, crockery, poetry, patchwork, etc.), these patients seemed being somehow relieved by their pain, preoccupation, and anguish. Consequently, I started to be actively involved in helping them by using some of my previous but small skills in drawings and poetry. Suddenly, the walls of the rooms in the ward (usually for isolation and confinement) seemed showing unexpected windows. Moreover, many patients started to write poetries or to paint canvas with spiritual subjects: Soul, God, Angels, etc. Practically, where possible, (walls, furniture, windows) their first artworks started to appear: paintings, flowers, abstract compositions, etc. At the same time, I thought: "That's it! The doors are open". We found a way to "escape from the ward". It was an unexpected and spiritual experience: those human beings, often unable to abandon their bed, seemed to find another "parallel dimension". No more in the ward, they could ride the wings of their fantasy to approach a less painful reality.

Practically this metaphysical dimension paralleled their artistic experience. Their enthusiasm helped me to replicate this experience, also because young hospitalized and very sick people confessed that by "drawing or writing poetries", they were able to overcome their nightmares and stress. Also, it was, for them, their spiritual will. A trace of their passage. Basically, a message of hope they wanted to leave to other human beings, filtered through years of lived sufferings, and during a present of reminiscences and insights. Many times, during the labs in Expressive Therapies, I could perceive in every suffering and sick person an inextinguishable wish: to stand actively, and in a decorous posture, in face of adverse life events, illness, and unbearable pain. This also means to find in the Self, instruments to continue to live in a meaningful way that, in the cases witnessed, also stands for being a "spiritual creator".

Practically, hospitalized men and women became able to generate something aesthetically important as a spiritual trace of the self, but also a message for others and parents. These aims animated the many painting and poetry exhibitions that I organized for many years, with HIV positive people and AIDS patients. In a word, in these client-artists, there was a sort of inner urge to recover a public image of the self through the artistic experience. In some cases, this task was facilitated by the fact that many young people victims of AIDS were already bearers of artistic skills. Consequently, they accepted soon my proposal to change the public awareness by entering through the "master doors". This also meant being able to talk to other people through a shared language: art. The exhibitions had, thus, a deep impact on the local culture. Regional painters and artists were willingly to exhibit their artworks, side-to-side with the paintings and poetries of people with AIDS. This way, many anonymous artists, who were previously hiding their nature of "ill people", were able to find a new value and self-dignity. Moreover, addressed as "artists" by other artists, they were proud to announce to the community to be the makers of several artworks. This was also a spiritual experience because reinforced communitarian bonds and feelings of connectedness.

The many times I have been involved in public exhibitions, conferences, AIDS awareness campaign, I have always noticed the deep spiritual bridge between paintings, poetries (some of which also from terminal patients), and observers/users. The messages, always of hope, were clear, and public opinion felt closer, as never, to these people. These experiences continued, and during the following years, while I was leading counseling sections for former drug users in a jail, I exported the same idea, and I started poetry labs for young prisoners. It was, also in this case, an enriching experience. The project named "Poetry in Jail", also in this case, served as psychic "evasion" and spiritual growth. The emotional and spiritual gain was the same. People were re-acquiring, through the art, self-dignity and a sort of pride in being totally themselves. Moreover, the poetry served as spiritual and emotional bridge between writers and readers. It was also the opportunity to remodel losses and mourning in order to find in the self a constructive but dormant side. In addition, on the part of the public that received these messages, also the same attitude was met: feeling closer to the artist, accepting him/her, feeling involved, and believing that humanity and richness can steam from unexpected venues and people.

Thus, my aim, mainly as a counselor, was always to create opportunities to help people to regain dignity when they felt it was lost. For example, helping terminal AIDS patients to have a space for thinking about colors and green landscapes when they understood that their hospital bed was perhaps their last dwelling. The effort was also to influence public awareness, and to make it favorable and closer to underprivileged people, when I felt the risk of community indifference or a pathetic attitude. As a result, the aesthetic bridge between artists and users served to fill emotional, cognitive, and spiritual gaps. Meanwhile, the aesthetic experience, directly applied to suffering and underprivileged people, helped them to increase self-esteem, sense of dignity, feelings of mastery, and satisfaction for the "accomplishment". These experiences were also exported into social centers for the homeless people, were I worked as volunteer. Here, too, I started sections of expressive therapies: through paintings and workable mud. During this project, I lead them to consider themselves not "deprived form life", but "enriched by their own experiences and losses". This was quite a cognitive restatement about the self. A sort of slogan of the kind "I am 'beautiful' especially inside". In fact, through the artistic experience, deprived people, poor vagrants, and clochards, perhaps for the first time, were able to recognize an unexpected and potential beauty in their life and soul. Slowly, during sections of expressive therapy, they started to acknowledge that all that "mess" in their life was, indeed, an important source to generate something important, beautiful, and spiritually pure and light. Moreover, through the artistic experience, they were able to talk with parish volunteers in a clear "inspired" way.

To well see, an important change for people who usually consider themselves as "being nothing and having nothing". Nothingness was soon moderated by canvas of simple but unexpected polychromy. Practically, the fatigue of a daily begging was magically abandoned during group sections for painting, poetry, crockery, etc. This, again, suggested the potential that arts have to join man to divinity, as Corinne Morel cites in her *Dictionnaire des symbols, mythes et croyances* (Arcipel, publ., 2004): "Art is frequently associated to spirituality, and helps to witness the majesty and greatness of divine beings".[57] Later, this project continued, and I started to work as a missionary psychologist in developing countries. Being appointed as supervisor for a children's foundation, I lived many years in South America, mostly in social and educational centers in suburban areas. Here, too, the artistic experience was present, and replicated with children from slums or *favelas*. In the missionary schools, children from underprivileged neighborhoods constantly received art sections and teaching, in this, showing particular mastery. In addition, expressive therapies helped them to have a sort of powerful instruments to give free access to their enormous expressive potentials.

For example, many school children were coming from violent families. They were often unable to use words to communicate their emotions. Thus, in these schools, the sight of children doing some sort of artwork was a constant encounter. Similarly, art also served as educational strategy to work with violent children, or youngsters free on parole that lived in family houses. Besides, in South America, I had the opportunity to appreciate the unique potential for artworks with recycled material, where all children showed a particular mastery. Art experience also plays an important role in those communities that face significant social deprivations and poverty. It is known the extended development of Religious art in Ethiopia. Here, religious topics, especially Christian iconography, practically enliven any artwork.

The deep experiences for which I am grateful to all these artists, have then helped me to make some reflections about the implication and the help that expressive therapy can bring to people in very delicate conditions, and being victims of: diseases, poverty, violence, deprivation, famine, terminal pathologies, etc. Practically, I gained a sort of insight about the potential on self-dignity, spirituality, and intelligence of people accepting to expose themselves by using expressive therapies. For instance, I perceive the deep impact that expressive therapies can have in the health maintenance and the recovery from chronic and debilitating diseases, and the potential of using expressive therapies and art counseling in hospitalized patients. In addition, I believe that expressive therapy can have an important impact for the care of terminal patients or underprivileged people or adolescents, who are constantly in a stage of finding a new and spiritual meaning to their own existence. Practically, during the sections of expressive therapy in hospital and in social centers, I could perceive in every suffering and sick person an inextinguishable wish: to live in an active, constructive, and dignified way life events, illness, poverty, pain. This cognitive and artistic reframing would, thus, help them to transform these experiences into a path for personal growth and meaning.

Moreover, in the places where people suffer (hospitals, care houses, social centers, etc.), the psychologists or the social assistants I met, always felt a deep wish to offer to clients (sick persons, homeless people, violated children) something more beyond a charitable and hearty welcome or a support psychotherapy. Besides, by acting as art therapist, I felt the importance to enrich any client (the very sick, the drug user, the homeless, the prisoner, the underprivileged child), and to help him/her to express the Self by preserving the importance of what "s/he was here-and-now". Furthermore, I prompted these people, through several art exhibitions, to gain a valuable place "in the world", and to overcome timidity, and a natural feeling of inferiority. For example, through art exhibitions, I was able to help the coming out of HIV positive people. For the first time, by presenting themselves as "art makers", they were also able to tell openly about their own disease. Many art exhibitions reinforced these positive results. Hence, an itinerant exhibition of artworks of HIV positive people was created, and presented during major thematic conferences. With the assistance of other health operators and nurses in hospital, we opened wide expressive-therapy sections in the wards.

This project helped hospitaliazed, but also external clients, to use their time to "create" paintings, poetries, small handworks, etc. What emerged was that the sublimation of pain and sufferings through expressive-therapy, allowed the bed-ridden patients to have some breaks from their obsessive fears and health preoccupations. Hence, I felt that by expressing themselves through the art (poetry, paintings, wood work, etc.), men and women coming from stressful life events were able to transform their present, their life history, their pain, from sad events and worries, into events fit to be sublimated into, and through, creative actions. In addition, as for any event involving mind, soul, and intelligence, also during the expressive-therapy sections, the emerging meaning was also spiritual and metaphysical. The same Kandinsky, cited Schumann: "Lighting up the depth of the human heart is the artist's task. The periods in which art does not have big men, in whom everyone misses the metaphorical bread, are spiritual decadence periods. The psychic energies are underestimated, if not ignored indeed".[58] The expression "metaphorical bread" used by Kandinsky, points out the metaphysical potential of the art, which is possible through a creation. This involves the possibility, for a person who suffers but who creates, of exceeding consolidated aspects of nature and world through creativity and meditation.

This way, a person limited in the physique or by pain, can penetrate a range of emotions not evoked by daily objects. Finally, across a poetry (or a painting), a patient can finally arrive to a spiritual dimension, that is unknown and emotional. Practically, it is spiritual also because emotional. Therefore, between the rhymes, the poet's "spirit" is poured. However, this is something that is knowable not objectively, but only through the language of emotions. This reminds us the meaning itself of "poem" which derives from the Greek word "poema" or "creation", and from the verb "poiéo" which means, "I create". Sometimes, the artist works with a lack of an external "object" that is, an outer reference. This way, a poet or a painter gains accesses to an emotional memory of his, often bypassing the visual memory. Furthermore, an artist directly draws from the own spirit, and, through fantasy and metaphorical exercises, can elude and sublimate the effects of a real model (a face, a landscape, a nature). In addition, spirituality in the art is also a shared emotional experience, a private and open dialogue between a creator and a user, between a sick person and society, a helper and his/her client. It can be, thus, a route for disclosing inner emotional turmoil or acquisitions, or to share the same "metaphorical bread", specifically, a spiritual experience.

Thus, for the suffering person, a spiritual experience acquired through the art, can represent the preferential strategy to relieve a painful existence. Nevertheless, the emotional gain is reciprocal. Not only is the artwork a "thing" of the artist. It also belongs to the user of the same who applies the art production to sound the own spirit. Consequently, if the spirit of a patient-artist has been delivered to a user, counselor, public, then, it would be their moral obligation to keep alive this human heritage.

To summarize, I believe that art and expressive therapy, have enormous implications during the spiritual growth of clients counseled. On the other hand, spirituality, emotions, and resilience can be strengthened through paintings and poetry, and art is an additional assistance offered to sick people and underprivileged population. Besides, art, especially sacred masterworks (religious paintings, music, and poetry), have always helped a man and a woman to accelerate their progression towards higher degrees of psychic complexity, and to improve strategies to overcome stress and pain. In fact, the artists' inner movement through the own rhymes and canvases can perfection their spiritual attitudes, their psychological resilience, and their coping skills for daily distress. In a certain way, expressive therapy can somehow parallel spiritual counseling. Other times, spiritual counseling can accept expressive therapy as a method for reaching a better healing and cure of the afflicted person. For example, the use of sacred art and symbolism encourages either the artist or the observer to make alternative reality testing, in order to achieve self-healing during pain, diseases, and stress. It would be, then, an interesting project to predict degrees and quality of mutual influence between spirituality, art, and stress. Practically, the question is: "Is there any connection, and of what degree, that would increase resilience and lower the threshold of physical/psychological pain when a client is undertaking sections of expressive/spiritual therapy?". Furthermore, "Can expressive therapy enhance body/mind connection (e.g., better health and faster recovery) in very sick people exposed to, or practicing, music, paintings, and poetries with a specific focus on spirituality and religious symbolism?". Finally, "Can I promote a certain degree of well-being by brief or prolonged exposition of sick people to artistic sections with a higher spiritual symbolism and iconography: e.g., participation to paintings with religious subjects; periodic and guided visits to sacred art exhibition; creation of artworks encompassing religious subjects; listening of sacred music, etc.?". Consequently, the question is: "Can the sacred art, intended either as exposition to and performance in, activate higher emotional and metaphysical functions, and help a person to a better health and healing strategies?".

The starting hypothesis is that both healing and creativity use common cognitive routes. In addition, art would reinforce imagination and meditation that are also at the basis for body/mind interactions and immune system activation. From here, the question: "Can the focus on the scared, reached through art, promote better health behaviors and strengthen the immune system?". The French philosopher Montaigne recommended the reunion between body and soul, and stated that the soul should "...join the body again, embrace it, fondle it, assist it, control it, counsel it, and correct it, until their works appear in agreement and uniform".[59] Thus, the inner change improved by the sacred art and the manipulation of sacred symbols, through the exercise of spirituality and expressive therapy, seems a viable method for dealing with a natural quest of humans, and, perhaps, a practical way to deal with suffering and stress. In fact, it is a sort of reading that a man or a woman who suffers would do in their soul in order to achieve higher degrees of insight, and a stronger resilience when facing diseases, poverty, isolation, or any other spiritual and existential threat. Finally spirituality in art can enhance strategies for meditation and reflection about the self, and through a symbolic and artistic experience, human spirit and body are reinforced.

3

Spirituality and ethics in the health settings

✦

3.1. THE RELATIONSHIP BETWEEN HEALTH OPERATORS AND CLIENTS

The relationship between physicians and patients is not always easy. Many patients often fear not to receive the best treatment. Sometimes, even not respected. Other times they do not feel encouraged in to set questions when diagnosis or therapy are not comprehensible. Alternatively, they complain about the quality of the relationship and the communication they had with several physicians and nurses. Let we see how to promote the spiritual and emotional rights of clients.

3.2. A RELATIONSHIP NOT ALWAYS CRYSTALLINE

The darkness in the spirit
creates clouds during
interpersonal relationships.

A person who crosses the threshold of a hospital or a private clinic might not posses the proper tools to appraise if the diagnosis that s/he will receive, or the therapy to which s/he will submit, is correct or the best. Despite this, with admirable trust, s/he puts his/her life in the hands of several experts. Beyond this, very few are able to establish if the physicians consulted have eventually mistaken their intervention.

Do you think that this is a rare case? And why? To err is human and physicians, too, might be wrong. Among health care specialists there is who has the humility and the intelligence to recognize it. However, there is also who persists in the error. During my personal experience, I found health operators not aware of their own mistaken approach to patients or, even if aware of it, and conscious, seemed ashamed to admit in front of their patients that they were not able to proceed in their performance in the most suitable way. Simply, sometimes, these health operators did not want to waste their time with clients.

Many patients complain about the quality of the relationship with hospital physicians or with other health care specialists. Anyhow, what would create conflicts with physicians and nurses? All the following. A traumatic communication often, and above all, when the health care specialist assumes a cold and authoritarian tone. The difficulty of a patient to understand the used medical terminology. The common stress from long waiting lists that intensifies, in a patient, the feeling of being no more important than a number or a schedule. A business like and a detached attitude of health care specialists during interpersonal relationships with clients. The lack, for a patient or counselor, of a comfortable setting, or a slender privacy (different from a waiting room or a corridor) where to be able to talk in all calm, without being interrupted by others, or from duties non tied up to one's own worries. The bad habit of some health care specialists to spread aloud the name of their patients and their pathology in front to casual listeners, especially in the waiting rooms: "Mrs. Brown, how is your ulcer today?". Scarce information received by a patient about the practiced diagnostic procedures, and about the effects of the therapies received. Impossibility, for a patient, to set some questions or, vice versa, the abstention from physicians to verify that a patient has understood the medical information delivered to him/her. Sometimes, some health care specialists accuse their patients for "not being able to understand 'simple' medical information". As a consequence, for a sort of reverential fear, and not to be considered "ignorant", many patients pretend to have understood.

Besides these reasons for attrition, there are others, mainly in the situation in which the illness is very serious. Practically, when sufferance is deep, and the feeling of abandonment is chronic, patients hope, and rightly pretend, that every clinical intervention, addressed to them represents the best available. In fact, in case of serious or terminal illnesses, patients fear that the consulted physicians do not have in reality a suitable professional preparation. Other patients know that there are city, nations, hospitals, or experts that for the same type of pathology get best results or, however, more encouraging outcomes. For patients or their relatives a situation becomes more unbearable, when they believe that a physician has wanted to intervene even when not having enough cognitive or professional elements to assure the best results. In this case, we talk about a "lack of delegation" by part of doctors.

Besides, many other patients complain that the consulted physician has not encouraged them to seek advice from other experts. In short, they do not feel facilitated in acquiring additional information useful to them to better understand and cure their own illness. Instead, when the relationship is ethical, patients are invited by physicians to consult other experts with the purpose to be able to choose, in full freedom and trust, how to proceed for taking care of themselves. In this happy case, health operators have implemented an ethical and spiritual approach with the full recognition of the human and spiritual part of clients and their needs.

3.3. PATHOLOGIES BORN BY A DIFFICULT COMMUNICATION

> *The wounds in the spirit*
> *come from unloving words.*

Every time that a person is worried about his/her own health, s/he becomes the target of a chain of emotional, social, spiritual, and philosophical events that influence his/her emotional reactions and resilience to the illness and its consequences. It does not care how serious a disease can be, behaviors for the promotion of health always tie to a search of sense in the own life. It is usually in these instants, a little before or shortly after a diagnosis of a serious illness, that the intervention of a helper becomes fundamental. Generally, in hospitals, the scenarios can change but not the emotional reactions of clients that are attended in them. Besides, each hospital is physically a system of chained actions where different operations are performed for the physical, psychic, and spiritual health of clients. The circumstances for the interaction with clients might change if we are in a private or public organization, but not patient's needs. Nevertheless, because of many incumbencies and duties gravitating onto doctors' and nurses' shoulders, it can be easy to "forget" some patients or to be fast during interventions that require, instead, pause and reflection. Therefore, any corner of a hospital, of an ambulatory, of a social center, even the less important and not strategically central, can host an emotional and anonymous spiritual crisis. Moreover, the tormented human being seeks for a concealed corner where to contact the inner self and where to pray.

Basically, it is spontaneous to believe that the worries for their own health occupy the first place among the fears of the human beings. This way the threats to health are a constant challenge to the sense of safety, of self-respect, of resilience of every person. In addition, for a patient, the acceptance of an unpleasant diagnosis is as shocking as accepting beautiful news after an endless ordeal of checks and therapies. Besides, living the hospitalization is so devastating that a psychological stress and a depression are normal.

Consequently, it becomes the task of any helper to increase in their clients their sense of autonomy, of comfort, of satisfaction in the health actions, and the compliance in the diagnostic and therapeutic procedures. Despite this, the users of the health layouts daily face a chain of micro-shocks and micro-stresses. This to the point that a clear vision of the real patients' needs becomes difficult, even if it is necessary to draw near to him or her in a psycho-bio-spiritual way. Besides, in patients worried about their own health, any attempt to give a sense to what is happening can be as strong as the impossibility of health care specialists to help them from this side.

At this point, the search of a meaning becomes prevailing and exclusive to the point that if the helper leaves a client without any psychic support, s/he can develop what I define as a chronic symptom of *Hospital Emotional Shock (HES)*. This way, even if subsequently the diagnoses or the therapies conclude with success, many patients show signs of HES because of the sequences of stormy relationships with several specialist figures in hospital: mutual incomprehension, up to interpersonal conflicts produced by a scarce preparation to the helping and the professional etiquette by some hospital employees. The wounds of one or many HESs show during following check-up visits creating a progressive deterioration in the trust for the hospital organization, and for the hospital personnel, even if in the following occasions these relationships are improved. This way, every time that a helper interacts with a patient or a client of the hospital, s/he will have to consider mainly three categories of people, all bearers of signs of past or actual HES:

- A patient that has suffered a past Hospital Emotional Shock, and that at the moment shows fear or scarce trust in the health personnel.

- A patient that is now neglected in his/her fundamental needs, and that is developing a HES.

- A potential and future patient whose emotional reactions, and whose trust in the hospital institution (and therefore the chance to develop a HES) depend a lot on the kind of relationships with which s/

he will be treated. This will also influence his/her compliance and resilience toward future health interventions.

Nevertheless, we now see what are the psychological characteristics of a HES:

- A *constant fear* of a patient that the own physician hides his/her scarce professionalism or that s/he decides to act despite of not being provided of enough experience for treating the introduced problem.
- A *hidden fear* of any patient that the health personnel can humiliate him/her if s/he had to show his/her own hesitancies, and his/her own perplexities around disputable methods and around unclear health procedures.
- A *marked anxiety* of any patient about being in the wrong hospital with unskilled physicians.
- A *deep depression* of a patient for not having enough economic and social tools to choose an alternative health structure for a better diagnosis and therapy.
- A *low self-esteem and feelings of guilt* in a patient for not succeeding in assuring to his/her own family, better hospitals and better therapies.
- A *phobia* in a patient that his/her own body suffers from some permanent handicaps because of interventions received by health care specialists without ethics and with a low professionalism.

Consequently, every time a helper faces a patient, s/he has to consider that in an implicit or hidden way this patient is animated from one or all the preceding fears. Therefore, the construction of trust, especially in a hospital or community, is central for accomplishing with success every other intervention of diagnosis and care. Moreover, everything is based on the sensibility of the helper and on his/her ability to reduce or to prevent a HES. This way the helper (any health care specialist can be a helper: physician, nurse, chaplain, each formed in the relationship of help) becomes an essential middleman among the overt or covert needs of patients, and the procedures of diagnosis and care. These interventions are basic for the reduction of anxiety, stress, and depression from hospital.

3.4. GENERAL NOTIONS OF HOSPITAL ETHICS

Feeling a total person,
means the same as
feeling loved.

Within job organizations, a hospital represents a place where, more than elsewhere, the relationship that is established among health personnel and clients is fundamental to allow a best service, and to establish a physical and psychic state of well-being in clients. In this chapter, we will use in a similar way the terms of "patient" that brings to the common representation of users of a health service, and the term "client". This last term implies that the person who enters a hospital expects to receive (because of the rights of citizen) a sequence of relationships, services, and "treatments" that usually is expecting anybody else as "client" of an organization or private service. To tell it in other terms, if a patient simply shall be "served and helped", then a client needs to be "satisfied". This radically changes the perspective of the ethical relationship with a patient of the hospital organization that, treated as a privileged client, becomes the central goal of the business mission itself. According to such perspective, the organization founded on this model, usually aims to produce in its own client-patients the maximum psychic and physical comfort with the purpose to increase their full "satisfaction". All of this is inserted in a sort of human and spiritual movement of the relationships that the organizations have with the own external (the hospital clients) but also internal clients (all the employees of the same hospital). To this, we can add that a "client's satisfaction" can become the organizational mission for excellence plus the ethical goal where, all the hospitals that pursue the well-being of each man and woman in their psychic-physical-spiritual wholeness are heading.

Returning to the humanized hospitals, whoever lives and acts inside their boundaries becomes "client", or rather a subject of whom the organization desires the greater comfort or the smaller discomfort. These people are customers, patients, family of patients, employees, physicians, nurses, chaplains, etc. In this way, "client" is every subject that belongs to the tangled but dynamic net of business relationships, until to include also the indirect clients that work for reason for their state or profession with or for the hospital: scientific informants, friend of patients, organizations of volunteers, etc. For this reason the ethics in hospital becomes also the ethics of the relationships inside the hospital. In this case, the fortification of hospital humanities rises and is produced through the creation of "good and beautiful relationships" among all the actors of the organizational life. However, just because the ethical organization turns to man in its wholeness, then the ethics of the relationship becomes the primary tool through which a hospital makes its own interventions effective. This is to affirm that without ethical relationships also the health interventions weaken and lose their effectiveness and credibility. Still reasoning more on this, we can also affirm that physical comfort, health, and recovery become possible only inside a relationship of a certain type between a hospital and its client, and such relationship has in itself the characteristics of an ethical and spiritual relationship. To this, we will try to give a certain type of physiognomy during the next lines.[60]

3.5. OF WHICH CLIENTS WE SPEAK?

Being rude to each other
breaks the spiritual cement
that keeps the world alive.

When we speak of organizational relationships, we also have the tendency to underline that the "master groups" of people who operate inside them (and, therefore, also inside the hospital organization) are mainly two: 1) the external client or real patient; 2) the internal client, represented by the employees of the hospital, and by whoever works for it, also if outside the premises. Then, these two groups tend to widen in concentric loops, therefore, the external client, can be also the family of a patient, its friends, its family physician, and whoever turns to the hospital to use the disbursed services. This way, a person who refers to a call center to make queries or to fix an appointment by telephone, is to full title "client" and, therefore, carrier of the same rights and requests of any hospitalized patient. For the goals of the ethical hospital this means that since client, we will need to use toward the customers of the hospital, the same care, and therefore the same ethical relationship and attention that we assure to the hospitalized patient, sick, very sick, or not yet to be, since not yet been born.

Same intensity of ethical relationships, and therefore the same moral attitude, shall be employed by the hospital for its "internal clients": physicians, nurses, auxiliary, technical, etc. In reality, to well see, anyone becomes "client" of the hospital, and anyone desires (as person bearer of human rights) to receive from a hospital that minimum respect that makes her/him feel a "satisfied client", above all on the side of human respect and of equitable treatment. However, the relationships amongst clients are so delicate that is enough that a client shows some resentment or nourishes the perception not to have received an "equitable" treatment, to find in him/her desires of retaliation toward the hospital that has not been attentive to his/her discomfort and reasons.

The dynamics of the ethical relationships in hospital is such that it is just when an organization introduces itself as a "model", that it also increases "the expectations of its own clients." In addition, everyone knows this phenomenon when clients/patients confuse the way of doing of the whole hospital with the way of doing of a health care specialist that has appeared less polite in their comparisons. In the fantasy of external clients or patients, who works for the hospital represents it. This way, if an employee of the entry appears impolite or hasty, then the client that has asked for information interprets this attitude as a way of doing of "the whole hospital". Moreover, if a physician interacts with a client in a little moral way, and with a business like attitude, for a client this is a sign that the whole hospital behaves similarly. Once the mutual incomprehension is born, it is just because the relationships with clients, in breast to the organizations, are so interconnected, that it becomes arduous to bring conflicting relationships between patients and hospital to the "state of normality." Letters of excuses are needed, disciplinary actions shall be performed, and a series of actions are essential to restore in the dissatisfied patients an acceptable level of trust towards the hospital.

Besides, always staying within the relationships among people, it is important to consider the concept of "membrane" that represents the "why" and the "where" such relationships happen, and the dynamics of the same ones when placed on the two sides of such membranes. In fact, by being a theoretical surface endowed with two sides –hypothetically the place where two people or two groups interact– it is also furnished of a certain permeability or impermeability, according to the quality of the relationship between the two people or groups of people. This way, a very permeable membrane allows a free flow of feelings and actions of support between the two sides. This becomes the optimal environment for spiritual growth and development. Contrarily, a semi-permeable membrane allows only some mutual actions, reducing, however, the quality the quantity of the relationships themselves.

In case of impermeable membranes, without "pores", it is as if two watertight compartments existed. The people or groups that practically interact are insensitive to what happens in the other side, to the matching part. For example, I see this happening in some hospital where there are interactions between doctors and patients solely aimed to underestimate the suffering and the comments of patients, and to treat them exclusively as "biological boxes".

In this way, operational models of relationships inside hospitals can be created each one with an own peculiarity as it regards the communication and the relationships among people. To start, we have two types of interactions between the two sides of the membrane that separates the internal clients of the hospital (employees, managers, doctors) from the external clients or real patients. According to the permeability of the membrane, the flows of communication and actions of support can mainly be directed toward the other side of the membrane, or to focus on the same side when between the two faces there is not a good communication and relationship. In case of a difficult interaction between the two sides of a membrane (doctors-patients), there is a difficult exchange among internal and external clients. Every group perceives to have difficult relationships with the counterpart. Therefore, mutual incomprehension and stress are generated by scarce relationships or by non-ethical relationships.

Figure 8 – A permeable barrier allows reciprocal directions of communications, actions of mutual support, and assistance (straight arrows) while, in case of impermeable barriers there is no opportunity for interaction between internal and external clients: doctors, nurses, and health operators towards clients and patients.

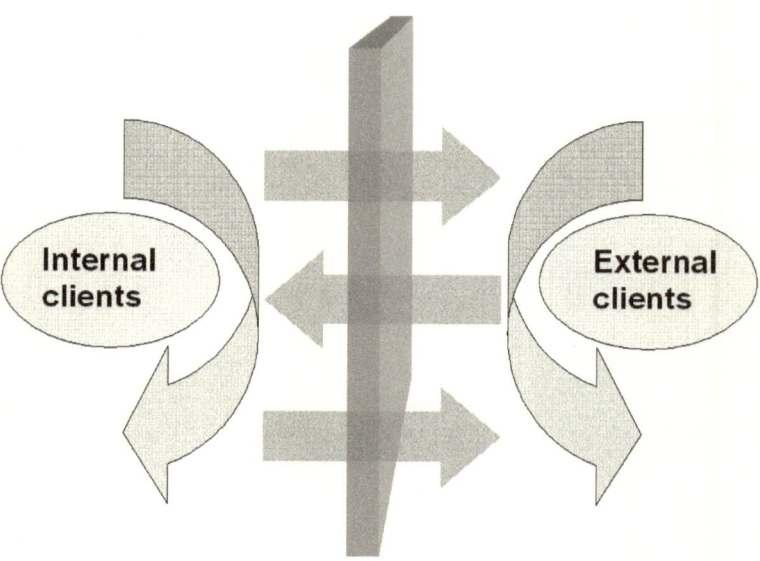

One impermeable "membrane" that separates clients amongst them, can be interpreted as an invisible barrier that is raised because of the natural or unintentional differences existing between the two sides, and therefore, between the two types of clients:

1. *Differences tied up to one's own role.–* That of physicians separated by that of patients. When a barrier becomes inaccessible to an exchange of roles, every person who participates in the relationship has difficulty to put on the shoes of the others since s/he does not know how one feels about living in the role of the counterpart. For instance, a physician does not succeed to empathize with patients who are carriers of a psychic suffering; similarly, a demanding patient does not succeed in understanding that his eccentricities slows down the operations of nurses.

2. *Cultural differences.–* In this instance, a barrier becomes more and more impermeable as the people involved in the relationship have evident cultural differences, above all tied up to the way of staying in a mature and moral relationship with the neighbor. The health personnel always prepared to do everything possible for who desires to be assisted, could have difficulty in interacting with antisocial young people who refuse and contest any type of intervention turned to their health. Here, spiritual counseling cannot be treated unless resistant patients become aware that "soul" and "spirit" are important issues in their life.

3. *Disparity in religion or value system.–* This becomes particularly evident in interpreting the meaning of life and the reason to stay alive or to die. Abortion, euthanasia, and other practice can be demanding for the doctors and nurses who do not share this point of view. In other cases, clients are bearers of ways of interpreting health and risk behaviors that do not take life and health as their primary concern. In all instances, entering the hospital also means sharing the idea that life and health, are a primary concern, and that behaviors that impede the full attainment of a good health are not accepted values for the health personnel. Moreover, patients that are familiar with risk behaviors and that show strong biases, might feel uncomfortable with anyone who is trying to be sensitive, delicate, and honest. Much depends on the way they interpret intimate relationships and interpersonal sharing. Moreover, some neurotic patients might revert roles and start to "spiritually educate" nurses and doctors.

4. *Differences of age.–* They can have an interesting significance when the relationship concerns a certain way of intending the culture of health, and the ways to have a greater comfort. For example, young health workers could be frustrated when they interact with an elderly person who seems having lost every interest in keeping on living although no serious pathologies in his/her health were found. Similarly, an elderly physician could live with frustration the fatalist vision of a young person who displays behaviors that put to risk his/her own health, or that lives issues related to religion and spirituality as a form of dogmatic obligation.

5. *Topographical differences.–* The barrier becomes almost impermeable if the people who interact in a relationship are physically and emotionally distant the one from the others. In fact, in order to settle an ethical relationship of mutual support (necessary for starting a spiritual assistance), we need a certain amount of physical proximity among the people who interrelate so that a mutual feeling establishes. Even if a client is physically far, the possibility to be able to communicate with him by telephone or e-mail reduces the emotional separation that the excessive distance creates, together with feelings of extraneousness. A physician that never visits his/her own patients in the room of the hospital or at home has created a barrier between him/herself and another human being, and is reducing the possibilities of ethical and spiritual relationships.

To return to the characteristics of the membrane, we can obtain the following options:

1. If a membrane is enough permeable, a bilateral and balanced flow on the two sides of it can be observed. The two sides (internal and external clients, doctors and patients, nurses and patients, health personnel with patient's family, etc.) interact in synchronous, egalitarian, and respectful way of the identity and the thoughts of the counterpart.

2. The pathologies in the relationships are born during semi-permeable barriers that create a unilateral flow of actions and information (Fig. 9). A patient or an external client simply becomes an "object" that must be studied but not considered as carrier of subjective, psychic, and spiritual demands. This can simply be a chalked behavior of the hospital and of its employees that have never thought about activating a reciprocal sharing with clients and their openings.

3. A semi-permeable membrane provokes a feeling of incomprehension on the side of the membrane that receives an action or information

without any possibility to answer (or to generate a feedback). For instance, a patient warns not to have "voice in chapter".

4. In the opposite side of a semi-permeable barrier, the most active of the membrane, a sense of tiredness can develop instead, born from the simple fact that either doctors or patients perceive to be always the more exploited, and feel the "overload" of unbalanced relationships in which there is not a bilateral exchange of actions of emotional support and communication.

A similar circumstance (Fig. 10) is found when the health personnel do not feel to have the opportunity to respond to clients' demands and communication. Often, in hospital, very problematic clients, especially when carriers of psychological and psychiatric problems, generate, on the health system, an overload of requests that go far beyond what is offered by the health system itself. Other times, with an underlying feeling of revenge, patients feel that everything is due to them without offering real opportunities to health personnel to interact in a mutual and spiritual manner.

Thus, in case of impermeable barriers, any communication between the two sectors is lacking. In fact, there is no possibility for helpers, health care specialists, physicians, and nurses to communicate with serenity with the counterpart, namely patients, their relatives, and every other client of the hospital. Similarly, also the external clients perceive a barrier when communicating to the employees of the hospital. Basically, patients perceive some mutual invisible obstacles between them and their primary caregivers. Thus, all the relationships are plastered, formal, and without excessive bilateral exchanges, and quite superficial. As a result, quarrels and open conflicts occur in these circumstances.

In case of conflicts, on one side of the interface, for instance inside the group of the internal clients (hospital organization, its employees, physicians, nurses), we witness psychic and social consequences either inside the group in conflict or inside the other interface, in the external clients, that are unintentional spectators or direct/indirect victims of the organizational conflict. In both instances, the foundations for iniquitous relationships and a decrease in operational efficiency of the hospital unities are produced. In this occasion, the barrier becomes *impermeable* because both the communication and the attention of a conflicting group are focused to its inside rather than on the demands of the own clients (on the other side of the membrane). In this instance, a spiritual approach cannot begin because all people have their mind concentrated on secular and daily issues, while spirituality is even dismissed as unfamiliar to what health workers consider to be "practical" problems of the ward or the hospital.

A similar semi-permeable barrier is raised when a patient does not want to furnish the truth, to cooperate, or is reluctant to communicate as he feels, and to enter in a true and deep relationship with hospital personnel. Sometimes, s/he does not want to provide the real version of the facts. In these circumstances, on the other side of the membrane this patient produces confusion and delays in the diagnosis and in the care. In fact, the health staff feels unable to start any counseling and spiritual support.

Figure 9 – A semi-permeable barrier allows only a unilateral flow of actions and communication while impeding a true exchange between the two sides, and the full expression of comments about what is said and done (in this case involving patients). The consequence is that the part that is in the receptive position is unable to give its own critiques and feedbacks, like many patients in hospital settings, while it also feels misunderstood. This circumstance lowers the ethical management of the system and the spiritual/psychological assistance on any external client and patient.

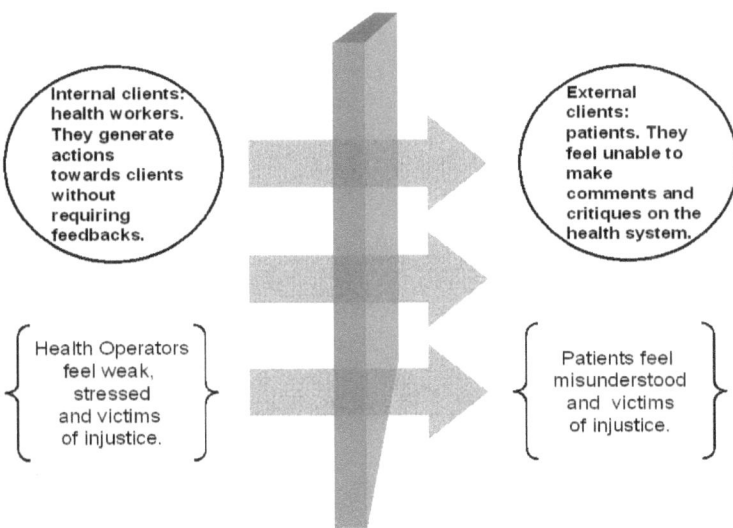

Figure 10 – A form equally similar to a semi-permeable membrane, with a unidirectional flow, sees the side of the patients as carriers of demands, requests, and needs that do not succeed in being satisfied for lack of personnel, or because the health personnel believes that they own needs are those to be underestimated (lack of specialist personnel, lack of equipments). On the side of the human interactions, the internal client (doctors, nurses, etc.) perceives itself as if it were deprived of communicative and interactive tools to cope in the best way with many and demanding customers.

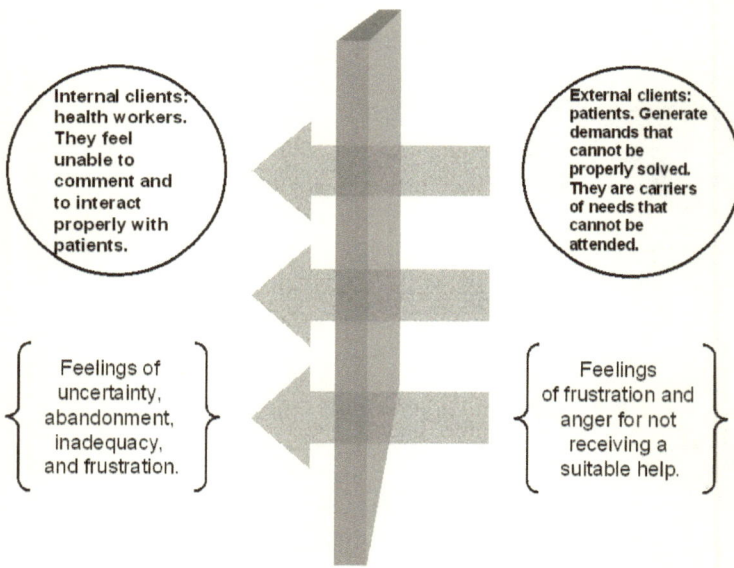

Figure 11 – A form of impermeable membrane is generated by conflicts inside one group. If it is the internal client that presents conflicts, then, errors in diagnosis and treatment are frequent, while in the other group, that of patients, we find feelings of fear and mistrust toward the hospital and its personnel. Conflicts in the internal clients, even if not directly involving spiritual counselors, will generate, in these last, unwanted interferences and will lower their freedom and attitudes towards "spiritual" issues and philanthropy. Practically, any pressure onto the person who is involved in spiritual counseling might lover any efficiency and efficacy of this approach. Therefore, we shall imagine a sort of "facilitating atmosphere" in hospital, able to generate, sustain, and promote spiritual counseling. Without this optimal floor, spiritual counseling is less effective and at risk.

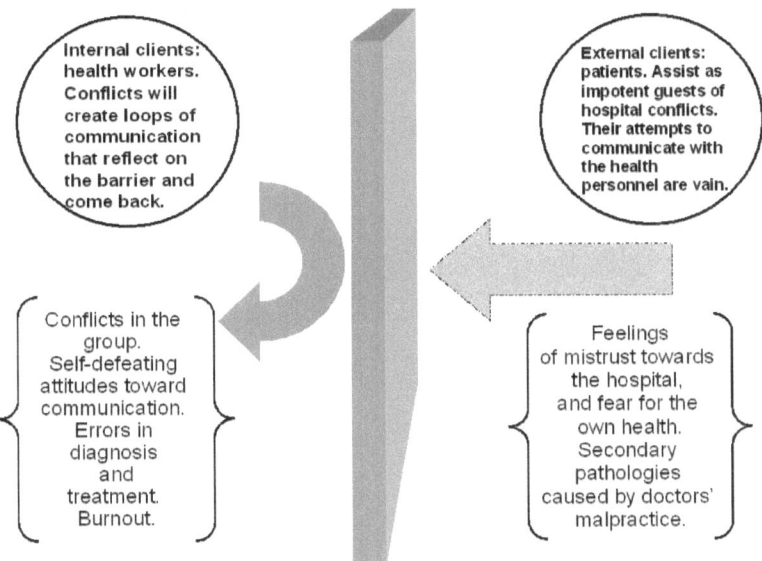

Figure 12 – When the problem is on the side of external clients or patients, mistrust towards health personnel would impede any exchange of emotions and the sharing during counseling sections. Here, a proposal of spiritual counseling by part of the hospital personnel is believed, by patients, as being unexpected and "not in tune" with their actual state of mind and intentions.

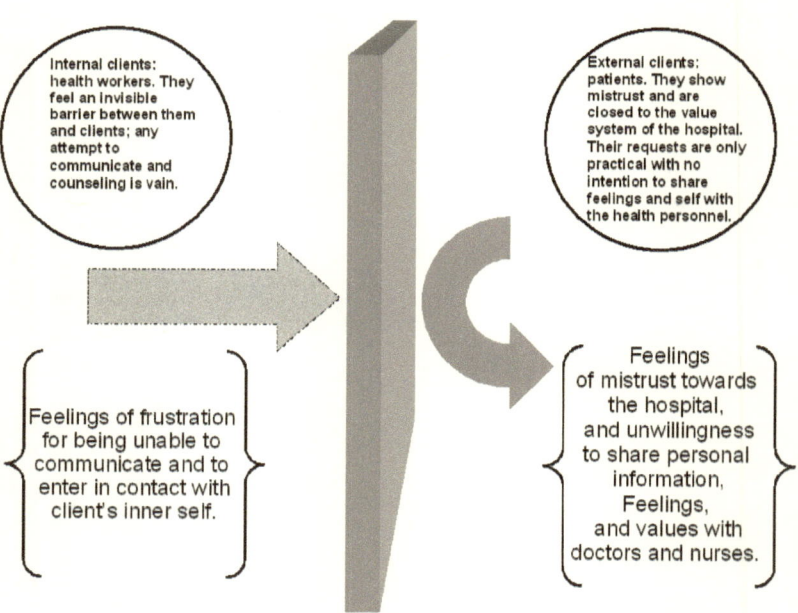

3.6. APPROACHING THE SICK PERSON IN A SPIRITUAL WAY

Listening in a spiritual way means taking care of the whole person.

To answer in an ethical way to the needs of patients means to stand always in a condition of positive listening. When a health care specialist is able to stand in a position of attention to the needs of its client, then, this last is able to render explicit what s/he desires. Although this is apparently simple, few times openings exist to make this happen. In fact, some hospitals always persist in their identity of "distributors of medical and surgical actions", while patients remain the "sick body" to whom such actions are addressed. Therefore, only physicians and nurses spiritually oriented become deep and desirous to talk after a quick "How is it going today?". Consequently, also patients forget the habit to disclose to physicians and nurses their desires, anguishes, fears, that good part play on the evolution of the illness and on clients' own psychic and physical balance.

To break with some ossified relationships, the ethical hospital proposes itself in a brave way to go beyond stereotyped relationships. Here, physicians and nurses understand that if they do not listen to the whole psychic-physical-spiritual person, few or no effect they will get from their medical and surgical therapies. Equally, a patient that enters an ethical organization learns, step by step, to read in him/herself because s/he understands that there exist people who want to and "know how" to listen to him/her. Thus, communication becomes the pivot to make to flow, in a bilateral way, actions of comfort between health care specialists and clients. In addition, and slowly, as that relationship deepens in the ethical hospital, we climb the steps of the evolution in the comfort of each single man: by promoting a physical comfort we generate a psychic relief, and by this last we finally aim to spiritual consolation. By now, in many hospitals, psycho-spiritual counseling is becoming the way with which every health care specialist, physician, nurse moves closer to his/her own patients in a holistic way.

Everything is born from accepting the point of view that either operating in a palliative care unit or in a simple outpatient ambulatory, the man/woman-patient is a being carrier of a triad of needs: i) a physical need: the own illness; ii) a psychic need: the fear not to survive, the idea of emptiness, and the fear of nothingness; iii) and, finally, a spiritual need: the perception of the self as being an entity that goes beyond one's own biological body to enter, instead, into a transpersonal and ultra mundane uniqueness.

This way the ethical hospital, through a skilled triangulation, sustains and strengthens these three poles of the comfort in an equal way, knowing that every pole gets some of its benefits from the adjacent ones: a physical comfort derives from an improvement of the psychic discomfort, and a substantial recovery is not gotten if the spiritual and psychic part of the sick person are not also attended. Some Authors comment that each person is a spiritual and physical being; spirit and body form a single nature.[61] Therefore, each "cure" shall be addressed to the three parts in order to obtain a single unitary effect.

3.7. PHYSICIANS AND NURSES AS "CLIENTS" OF THE HOSPITAL

Spiritual counseling
is nourished
by a respectful acceptance
of other's diversity.

In the ethical hospital, an alternation in the client roles happens. Therefore, also physicians, nurses, health assistants, etc., are carriers of their own desires towards the hospital. Alike their own patients, also doctors and nurses want to be treated as people and to become beneficiary of moral actions from the organizational milieu. This way, the cogwheel of the business ethics sees a very narrow gear among comfort of the internal clients (physicians, nurses, and other health care specialists), and the well-being of the external clients (patient, clients, family, family doctors, etc.). The transmission belt of this comfort is so intermingle, that it is enough that in the internal client appears the perception of iniquitous treatment from the management, that a negative downward flow is produced, actually to meet the defenseless patient of such health care specialist. Nevertheless, it is also true that the promotion of business ethics asks for a moral and human appointment of the health care specialists as first actors. The physical presence of physicians that spend their time in personal affairs while clients are crowding their waiting rooms, are conducts that the organization promoting ethical relationships cannot miss. In fact, if the physician is disinterested or angry at the hospital and the conflict is not resolved, then the human cost is high, too high, and any action to promote a holistic health of patients cannot take place. At risk it is the life and the health of the patients, including children, the elderly, the poor and abandoned people.

Thus, a sick hospital shows tangible signs of such discomfort, from the unsociable and discourteous relationships of the health care specialists toward clients, to the long waiting lists for vital diagnosis, to feelings of injustice and abandonment in the sick person, some of which dying. Here, the humanity and the brutal game in the corridors and the wards aims only to furnish the least necessary with the smaller work for the one who distributes the service, and with a constant attempts to elude every control or direction of improvement of the service. These are the "ghost-hospitals", a sort of sailboat adrift in a sea with vanished contours. Here, we cannot speak about ethical business, but simply of "wandering islands" where an own inside logic is in force, where each one dictates its own rules, and where we find a boat of people who row in decomposed or opposite way.

3.8. THE PRACTICAL VALUE OF THE BUSINESS ETHICS

The ethical organization
is a spiritual home
creating interpersonal efficacy
and intrapersonal wisdom.

If a hospital does not promote ethical and aesthetical relationships, "beautiful and good" encounters, then, there is a suffering on the side of "*efficiency, efficacy and cost effectiveness*" (the "3E", classical points for business excellence). These are the focus of many business executives, and a leading rule in ethical organizations, where the "3E" have the opportunity of showing all their importance on the side of the economic and human management of patients. We still remember the interconnection of different hospital services, and of the relationships amongst clients, that are the visible aspect of such services. Then, how does the ethics connect itself to the excellent management of the hospital on the economic side? A first answer is: *there could not be a hospital, successful in its services and with reduced human costs in absence of ethical relationships amongst all the subjects that live and operate within the boundaries of the hospital.* An example? If only one single employee of the hospital is dissatisfied with the treatment that receives from the management, then s/he will meditate to emotionally detach himself/herself from the hospital and to mind only to his/her "own business". Usually these "own business" carry high organizational costs: for example, using the whole day to visit personal web pages, using for one's own needs organizational goods and facilities, progressively subtracting small objects (pencils, papers, etc.), till showing a façade of cold indifference to patient's plights. It is what takes name of "loss of the psychological contract" when it is still present the "legal contract". In addition, with a patient the same happens. If a patient feels abused, s/he gets sick more, his/her symptoms worsen, s/he tries to get more attention from the medical personnel, and finally develops a series of "unexplainable" pathologies that are, in reality, his/her unconscious reaction to the perception of being misunderstood and a silent cry for help. All of this is translated in additional costs for the hospital with modest or negligible results on the improvement of the state of physical/psychic/spiritual well-being of that patient. For such reason the promotion of ethical relationships inside the hospitals turns itself into a transmission belt able to generate a total organizational comfort both of the internal and of the external clients, with a reduction in the human cost of the job, in organizational conflicts, in the dispersion of human and economic resources, and with an increase in the efficacy and efficiency of the medical-surgical interventions being equal the human and financial resources employed.

Thus, the milestones for promoting organizational ethics and a spiritual organization are:

1. What keeps alive the health system is the possibility of a constant flow of bilateral exchanges of well-being between internal and external clients. There cannot be a full attendance of patients and a transmission of well-being if also patients do not reflect their personal well-being onto the health personnel. Therefore, doctors, nurses, helpers get a greater amount of well-being as long as they are able to reflect this well-being to their own clients, and vice versa. *A mutual exchange of personal well-being is at the basis of a psycho-spiritual approach to health clients.*

2. A conflicting organization lowers the chances of ethical behaviors, while a successful organization is able to produce a higher rate of client's well-being with a lesser degree of labor and efforts. Practically, spiritual and psychological counseling are ways of standard behaviors of health organizations that are found in a surplus of wealth on the side of human interactions, and organizational values.

3. In ethical organizations, the interpersonal relationships are equally "beautiful and good", this meaning that the aesthetics of the interpersonal interactions is the visible part of a spiritually oriented approach in the health system. Indeed, there could not be spiritual

interactions without the perception that these relationships are also "attracting" on the side of human values.

4. Any human organization oriented towards the spiritual and psychological support of people, will also be recognized by the existence of "attracting" interpersonal relationships.

5. Greek philosophy would support the theory that "good things are also beautiful". Ethics and aesthetics stay together. Therefore, an aesthetical evaluation of spiritual relationships cannot be missed in ethical hospitals.

6. The absence of attracting and good relationships increases the degree of organizational conflict to the detriment of offering full spiritual and psychological assistance to clients.

7. At the same time, the reduction of ethical/aesthetical relationships increases the rate of diagnostic mistakes and improper medical and psychological therapies. Usually, malpractice is a hallmark of organizations not developed with ethical/aesthetical values.

Figure 13 – The flow chart of the organizational well-being. A health(y) organization responding to a code of conduct partly can be identified as possessing the basis for a spiritual approach to patients. Usually, the code of conduct ethically based, is the starting point to put each person, patient, and health personnel, at the center of the attention. A higher organizational efficiency and efficacy obtained by, and promoted by, positive interpersonal communication and mutual support, is a paramount also for a better diagnosis, enhanced therapeutic effects, and faster recovery rate in diseases. If these are the effects on external clients or patients, also health workers are favored by this climate. The general infusion of optimism will generate an enhanced workplace climate, will lesser complains, and will reduce the human costs of a job. These effects also increase the quality of interpersonal relationships amongst all the interacting people: patients, doctors, nurses, psychologists, health operators, etc. In other words, there could not be a spiritual attention to the sick person without improving the code of conduct of the hospital where this person is welcomed.

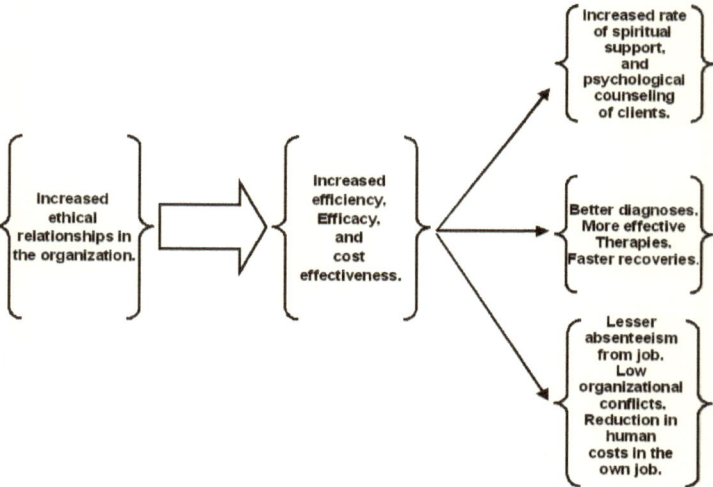

Figure 14 – A circular (recursive) model of the organizational well-being. It considers every point of the net of interpersonal relationships as a pivot generating comfort. For instance, the succession I/II/III proposes that a satisfied client, because it has obtained an efficient service, transmits this comfort of his back to the health personnel. This last increases its own optimism and improves its own predisposition to the ethical and spiritual treatment of clients. This process produces a greater efficiency that is translated in a good service to clients. The succession i/ii/iii would interpret as starting point the organizational efficiency/efficacy and cost effectiveness as promoters of increased client's well-being. This last would infuse optimism onto the health personnel that would finally raise its own job performances. The last succession A/B/C puts at the center of this virtuous circle the attitude of health personnel and their willingness to operate with joy and peace. This approach increases the organizational efficiency and efficacy with a final result in an enhancement in client's well-being.

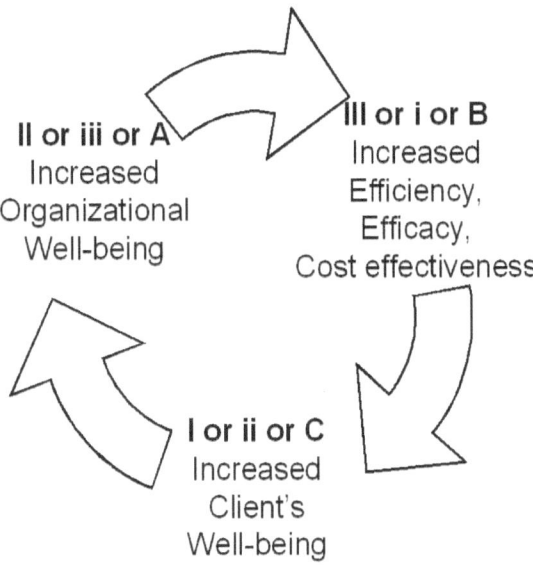

3.9. OBSTACLES IN THE INTERPERSONAL CODES OF CONDUCT

Spiritual assistance is
a gentle dance
of two renovated souls.

Since now, we have considered that an ethical relationship in the hospital has the opportunity to manifest itself, and to sustain itself as long as a constant and bilateral flow of relationships are maintained, and stamped on a mutual respect between the health personnel and the clients of the hospital. Practically, all these actions consist in a bilateral transmission of comfort by enacting any health behavior: therapy, diagnosis, assistance, help, etc. Usually, an efficient hospital and its personnel try to lift the sick person from his/her discomfort, and to establish a greater comfort. Nonetheless, a shared bias is that by dealing with specific organic illnesses and pathologies, the diffused medical model practically sees a physician as a sort of *problem-solver*. In other words, s/he is commonly perceived as a sort of solver of a biological rebus (anamnesis of the introduced problem), in order to deliver back to the patient a specific diagnostic-therapeutic answer. However, in the holistic hospital, spiritual and biological therapies are not so clearly disjoined. In addition, the flow of actions and well-being, as we have seen, are bilateral, and patients and doctors, try to enter into a flow of interactions that incorporate opportunities for a "bilateral" growth and development. Thus, we should imagine the strategies for a spiritual counseling of the sick person as usually staying on two important pedestals: *the giving and the taking*. Practically, the whole ethics of interpersonal exchanges, making the basis for the caring of the sick person and for its spiritual comfort, are variations in the strategies of giving and taking: each partner of the interaction offers specific give-and-take formats to create relationships that develop according to their basic ethical and spiritual principles (Tab. 1).

Table 1 – Strategies of Spiritual Counseling according to a bi-dimensional model of giving/taking.

Strategies in spiritual giving (usually in the helper)	Strategies in spiritual taking (usually in the helped)
With love and beauty.	With thankfulness and love.
Focusing always on the companion's needs.	Focusing on self in relation with others.
Using words to promote higher well-being.	Using words to express and to accept intimate dynamics.
Listening to clients as a way of promoting their self-discovery.	Listening to the own self as a way of enhancing self-discovery.
Appraising the own professional resources to help a patient in the discovery of meanings.	Appraising the helper's resources in the effort to discover meanings.
Using metaphors to ease the comprehension of difficult topics.	Using helper's prompts for anchorage to simplicity and clearness.
Using physical/emotional proximity to enhance mutual sharing.	Accepting physical/emotional proximity as a pathway to togetherness.
Enhancing informal thought as a way to interpersonal sharing.	Giving up the quest for a "business like approach" in the search for meanings.
Promoting client's autonomy and its spiritual intelligence.	Accepting an internal locus of control as instrument for the focal enlightenment in the spiritual growth.

How to say? A sort of role-play to which few people today would feel to object. Despite this, the ethics of the relationships, for their inner characteristics, implies that this model is more dynamic and equitable. In the sense that the hospital acting with rigidity does not stimulate, accept, or requires that the patient furnishes his/her opinion on what is happening. The question, "How do you feel"?, is not another technical investigation together with a verification of the kind, "Does this satisfy what you are expecting from us"?.

Actually, by acting in an ethical and spiritual way during the relationships, a physician stimulates an answer back from his/her own patients. Moreover, an "ethical and spiritual" doctor or nurse asks to their patients their own version of facts. Practically, doctors and nurses verify if patients possesses important information for their own comfort. However, above all, any helper, doctor, nurse puts into effect mechanisms of "feedbacks of return". In other words, a health worker always makes sure that a patient is not a simple "object" under observation but, instead, an active and co-working subject, cooperating with the health personnel to reach a common goal: "A good state of spiritual/psychological/physical health". All this implicates a greater freedom in the client to furnish "in real time" his/her own version of the facts, but also his/her own opinion on what is emotionally happening in him/her following the interventions disbursed in the hospital: therapy, diagnosis, etc. Why then not to equally hold informative and important the fact that a patient is tired of long cues, and the fact that s/he does not feel attended, listened, and understood?

By making light on this, we reduce the motives for conflicts and resentments in the hospital clients that often accept, passively, a game of the roles where it is missing, from the hospital, the application and the quest for "feedbacks". Therefore, the game of the roles, of the kind "tell me what you have and I will tell you what therapy to do", inhibits the understanding of a deeper suffering of the man and woman that get sick. This behavior can cause "ancillary pathologies" that emerge spontaneous in the unattended patients, and that are mysterious for both patients and health personnel. Practically, a patient feels misunderstood, weak ring of unilateral relationships, a little involved in to communicate if what the hospital is furnishing him or her really responds to his/her emotional, psychic, and physical needs. Moreover, from here, a sense of injustice received develops in patients. On the other hand, the health care specialists feel a psychic weakness according to this unilateral model of the "Tell-me-so-I-do". For example, in a research conducted by Canadian psychiatrists emerges that 53% of patients feel that it is important that spirituality is taken into consideration by their primary caregivers.[62]

Thus, the medical and nursing personnel that act according to this unilateral model, feel "overloaded" of job, exhausted, and equally perceives a sense of injustice since (alike their clients), they do not have the opportunity of rendering explicit to others their own discomfort, tied also here, to their own consolidated professional roles. The question is: "If the physician and the nurse are responsible of the patient's comfort, who is responsible of the well-being of the physician and the nurse?".

In conclusion, in the ethical health organization, where a spiritual philosophy is promoted, both internal and external clients, that is, health personnel and patients, have the same amount of personal value. Just because any spiritual interactions and spiritual counseling are a "mutual" and equal exchange of emotions and values, then, there cannot be gaps in the values system, codes of conduct, and personal worth. However, we shall always remember that possible lacks in spiritual care and understanding derive from a small training of health operators to deal with sensibility and knowledge with issues linked to spirituality.[63]

3.10. WHEN THE WHOLE HOSPITAL FEELS "UNDER PRESSURE": THE SECOND ETHICAL OBSTACLE

Spirit means "air", lightness,
a panacea for any pressure and load.

In order to promote the full development of ethics in hospital, each of the actors of the relationship, "internal and external client", should understand to be both carriers of certain rights but also subject to certain obligations. Here, the word "obligation" always implicates the way of drawing near to the relationship by respecting the counterpart. Moreover, the hospital and its personnel understand the importance to act in a moral and correct way towards the sick person. In fact, according to the optics of the renewed hospitals, also the external clients, entering to belong to a widened community, that of the ethical hospital, learn that there are some rules of respect of other people met here: practically, all the employees of the same hospital. Instead, a discourse on equity in the relationship, and on mutual respect could not begin if we skipped to consider that to promote a free bilateral flow of comfort (from health care specialists to patients, and vice versa), then also a client of the health service will need to have clear some limitations. These last are set him and are essential to the medical and nursing personnel to be more incisive in their work of assistance.

Consequently, the "second ethical obstacle" is found every time a patient is carrier of a request that is distant from a real and personal need, but that, instead, exceeds the real and concrete possibilities of the health structure to handle the same claim. In fact, there are some patients that use their own illness or their own discomfort to practice unbelievable pressures on the medical and nursing personnel and, at times, to get secondary advantages that stand aside from an ethical relationship between a hospital and its clients. For example, it can be found for young drug addicts that turn to the health system solely for "having methadone", or for homeless people who, in some countries, become quasi-permanent tenant of hospital premises. Therefore, during conditions of human desperation, waiting rooms and other corners not easily accessible in the hospital, become, then (and unfortunately), the place of "residence" selected by the suffering person who has been abandoned from everybody: family, society, community.

Therefore, a hospital, with its antiseptic, heated and protected environments, becomes the last or only dwelling for many people who have lost everything, and that know that the only pass for not "being sent away" is, in this case, the existence of "some illness." However, in a spiritual environment, and for the person in search for a spiritual and psychological assistance, also desires change, and the need for assistance becomes interchangeable with the need for protection. Besides, some people, those who feel deprived, and with few economic and community resources, would rather like to have much protection instead of aiming to obtain that assistance that is chronically withdrawn from them. Then, what we usually see, is that, according to the level of personal tragedy, people change their requirements, depending on the opportunity to get or not a practical help or good. Virtually, those who are convinced that there will not be any resolution to their quest, but that are also spiritually oriented, also change the quality of their needs that become more and more interpersonal. Thus, the need to have an identity, which is usual in each of us, in the underprivileged person, becomes a need for feeling helpful, which meets the need of affiliation and recognition. As we go along the several steps of spiritual development, all the *needs based on having become needs based in being*. According to this transformation, we get a complete metamorphosis of those needs we find in a normal condition. Sometimes, people in painful states, who are ill, continue to suffer because unable to transform "having" needs in "being" needs. Basically, by coming from conditions of chronic deprivations, they always seek practical resolutions to their problems by grasping as much as they can. This behavior does not promote, instead, a deep insight and, in effect, it puts a lot of overload of work onto the health operators. In this case, a patient makes pivot on his/her own condition of minus asking to the hospital the impossible one. Moreover, here it becomes incomprehensible to really reach what a client wants, since s/he is a carrier of a private project of life, that unconsciously boycotts every attempt of "a better life and of a better health". Consequently, the emotional results of the picture just seen are comprehensible. On one side, there is a patient that feels carrier of needs not shared by the hospital. At the same time, the health workers develop a sense of uncertainty and abandonment for not succeeding in being effective toward such a needy client. Also here, the moral pact is broken amongst hospital and patient, and a resolution of the impasse can happen only with a decision to consider a process of acculturation of the client to the moral rules, and to the model of which the same hospital becomes carrier.

Table 2 – Transformation of needs according to the degree of personal discomfort and tragedy. The transformation is also a sign of progression towards a higher degree of spiritual complexity and healing.

Practical Needs	*Spiritual Needs*
Need for having	Need for being
Need for protection	Need for feeling helpful
Need for action	Need for socially oriented actions
Feeling free to talk	Feeling inclined to listen
Need for expansion	Need for containment
Need for emotional movement	Need for emotional reflection
Need for personal growth	Need for collective growth
Need for privacy	Need for sharing

3.11. PROBLEMS INSIDE A SINGLE GROUP: THE THIRD ETHICAL OBSTACLE

Your first priority
is your neighbor's well-being.

A speech about ethics and spirituality of hospital organizations also implicates a thought about the dynamics of the relationships inside every pole of the interacting groups: health personnel and patients. Besides, organizational conflicts inside every group can be normal and accepted in many hospitals. Physicians and nurses that do not collaborate, or that even "quarrel at the presence of patients" is, at times, a scenario existing in many hospitals, also excellent. Nevertheless, a dynamic law of the organizational conflicts exists: whenever we find interpersonal conflicts inside the personnel of the organization, this fact also jams the relationships with clients. Besides, the conflict internal to a group lowers the efficiency and the effectiveness of the health organization itself. This way, if two nurses or two doctors use the hospital to bring forth a proper interpersonal conflict, it is the whole hospital that suffers and, in a more direct way, patients. The organizational conflicts that see involved the health personnel, produce, in the weakest rings, (and in those people who instead pursue professional and ethical goals) feelings of burnout and easy diagnostic-therapeutic errors. In other words, the quarrels among the boundaries of the hospital, the resentments amongst people, "are dangerous", "off-limit", really a block in the process of spiritual growth of the whole structure.

In short, it is like to attack furiously and randomly the control panel of a nuclear plant! This way, for a patient that presages this, that perceives that something among the people who work in the hospital must be twisted, it is as if it assisted to the conflict of the primary caregivers that represent, in the hospital, his/her parental figures.

Consequently, this patient develops a sense of fear. Stated in other words, a conflict in hospital, inside the personnel, produces in a patient-observer the idea to have submitted his/her own health to "unreliable" people, so deep is the wound that is born in who (all patients) has put his own life in the hands of others. This fact lowers or cancels the trust in the hospital, and produces in a patient the desire of escape or a feeling of mortification, that matches more or less the thought, "Look what comes upon me!". Practically, when an organizational conflict exists, there is little space in the mind of the physician or the nurse that feels depressed, mortified, and abused, to be serene and effective during spiritual counseling towards his/her own patients. Instead, here, errors in the diagnoses and in the therapies are more frequent. In fact, the health care specialist's mind is "distracted" and absorbed by interpersonal conflicts; this practically replaces his/her own priorities. Consequently, clients are no longer their main concern. Equally, a patient who faces a health care specialist discouraged and distracted by his/her own professional problems, feels also distracted. Therefore, both health care specialists and patients land in the no man's lands, in the Earths of nobody, where none knows anymore about what s/he is speaking about, and what s/he is doing. Spirituality and spiritual approach, here, become impracticable, and foreign to the shared values and attitudes.

4

The philosophy of spiritual counseling

◆

4.1. WHY SPIRITUAL COUNSELING

You can't feel "spiritual"
if you don't live "spiritually".

Spirituality in psychotherapy and counseling is becoming the new venture and challenge for many helpers, counselors, health operators, and psychotherapists. In this chapter, we shall see how to reconciliate two aspects that were kept separate or independent by former psychology: spirituality and psychology. Spirituality has become one of the most discussed topics in the new psychology and psychotherapy, yet we still need to draw principal theories about how one influences the other: psychology and psychotherapy. The question is: "Is coexistence of psychology and spirituality possible?", and "How?". The central focus still remains man in its unity, including the three main routes already identified by other Authors: Mind, Spirit, and Body. For a practical reason, the body of spiritual counseling will focus on Spirit and Mind. In the realm of the spiritual self, we will then position meanings, values, and spirituality, all applied to the existential part of all humans. On the other side, we shall locate in the psychic self, feelings, emotions, thoughts, and behaviors, as they relate to the objects of psychology, traditional counseling, and psychotherapy. At this point, during spiritual counseling, we witness the encounter of two persons: health worker and client, each one carrier of a psychic and spiritual part. From here on, each member of the dyad will be able to influence the other through one of the two parts, mind and spirit. In other words, *the therapist will influence the clients through conscious or unconscious operations on mind and/or spirit, while, the client him- or herself will influence the counselor through the own psychic and spiritual part.* The objects of the psychic part (emotions, thoughts, and behaviors) of the therapist, but also of the client, are found to cross-influence the objects of the spiritual part of the other party (spirituality, meanings, and values). This process is a flip-flop course of actions, dynamically evolving during the entire development of a therapeutic encounter.

Psychic part of a therapist ↔ Spiritual part of a client
Spiritual part of a therapist ↔ Psychic part of a client

This also means that certain values and spiritual contents (overt and covert) of the therapist will be able to exert specific modifications in thoughts, feelings, emotions, and behaviors of the client. And vice versa. A strong spirituality in a client might be able to exert some positive effects on cognitive and behavioral processes of the counselor. Basically, this becomes a striking happening during the encounter of health operators with patients (or their family) in hospital, when these people show unusual emotional energy deriving from their religion and faith. Another example, where we find a cross-over between spirituality/psychology/counselor/client, is when an empathic (behavioral and emotional self) counselor is able to elicit specific insights (meanings) of the client within his or her own existential goals. This process, because dynamic and bilateral, is a sort of transmission belt. The "healed client" becomes able to mirror counselor's attitudes, for example, by becoming more indulgent towards other fellows. Or even more. A spiritual counselor, respectful of clients' identity (values), and who holds a clear philosophy about life and meanings, can make clients feel understood and cared, with positive emotions and behaviors. The final occurrence is that the each subject, a client but also a counselor, would act on one part of its own identity (spiritual or psychic) in order to change the other part of the self (psychic or spiritual). It is the situation where an increased investment in the spiritual part of a person, would lead him or her to gain a major insight also into the cognitive and emotional parts of his or her own behaviors. Practically, this is the main venue for self-healing and resilience.

During spiritual counseling, usually a client reaches a self-healing through insight (personal) or help (interpersonal, e.g., counseling). In addition, this process can be more or less rapid depending on the level of development of the spiritual part of that client. Nevertheless, having to translate all these passages into operational strategies, a spiritual counselor shall decide where to act and when. In fact, there can be "easy" clients who only need a spiritual reinforcement, while others might need a more exhaustive and articulated process of spiritual counseling, because this part of the self is poorly developed. In any instance, it is not how deep and developed the spiritual part is, because what matters is the disposition and awareness of a client that this part (the spiritual side of the self) is present, valuable, and viable for reaching a better understanding and well-being. There are, for example, people who are very religious but who live existential losses and crises with a deep sense of religious abandonment and guilt. While others, who never claimed to be religious and spiritual, are instead able to reach valuable spiritual and religious insights just during moments of existential crises. Practically, I feel that *what is central is that a client understands and accepts diseases and death as natural and unavoidable parts of the own life. Therefore, any attempt to dismiss this as being the core point of the present or existential distress and crisis, solely slows down the process of healing and understanding*. For example, it is not rare to meet people who loose their faith during life crises, while others who reinforce their devotion during the same occasions.

Table 3 – Crossover between spirituality and psychology in counselors and clients.

Spiritual objects	*Psychic objects*
Spirituality	Cognitions
Meanings	Emotions
Values	Behaviors

4.2. THE PURSUIT OF HAPPINESS IN SPIRITUALITY

*The conclusion
of a spiritual search
becomes the beginning
of a new discovery.*

Usually we like to link joy to a true and full spiritual life. Actually, there are researches that show that people who are churchgoers, that pray a lot, and that refers to the Bible or other Holy Scripts for answers, are usually happier than those who do not show these traits. For this reason, spirituality and religion seem offering words of relief from daily strain and stress, and the suggestions coming from religious writings are, for most people, a true guide for life and a reliable way to reach a satisfying existence. Even though we have talked so far about sick people, there is an important link that binds people with serious diseases to people with miserable lives. When we think about a very sick patient, we must refer to a *reduced life expectancy*, while, when we talk about underprivileged people, we speak of a *reduced existential expectancy*, because linked to people with very low chances to survive in a decorous or human way (like refugees, people living in war areas, dwellers of slums, etc.).

Nevertheless, either in one case or in the other, emotional reactions to this shortness have a direct impact on the quality and quantity of joy, to the point that the quest of happiness often is a motivating drive towards spirituality and a spiritual life. Consequently, we shall make an important introduction to any other factor determining happiness in a man or woman and how this is linked to a spiritual explanation. This renewed criticism of old theories of happiness, shall thus reinforce the implication, if any, of spirituality in these happy factors. In other words, by discovering that friends and family are the main sources of happiness compared to money and business, we might also hypothesize that it is the spirituality of the family and the spirituality of friendship, with their imagined implications, that cause happiness.

For example, Kamman and Campbell reported that happiness arises either from a halo effect among "good things of life" or an overgeneralization from vivid short-term to pallid long-term effects.[64] Rimland demonstrated that selfish people were less happy than unselfish people.[65] Overall, there seem to be neuro-physiological changes of our body in response to happiness. For example, the exposition of happy faces to college students was correlated to a deceleration of heart rate[66] that is known to be a sign for a decreased psychic excitement and less anxiety. Moreover, Davidson and Fox demonstrated that there was a greater activation of the left frontal cerebral area when 10-month-old infants were exposed to videotape segments of an actress generating a happy or sad facial expression.[67] In a study of Tatarkiewicz emerged that science, art, and religion can be sources of happiness if they are the objects of unselfish interests, while also success in interpersonal relationships is another source of happiness.[68] Thorndike (in Tatarkiewicz) reported that amongst the factors of contentment it could be cited the satisfaction with various social needs, such as friendship, membership in organized groups, serving others.[69] Always for Tatarkiewicz, according to Saint Augustin it is happy the person who "is able to reach God", "Deus qui haber, beatus est".[70] The modern school of Aristotle's philosophy affirms that the aim of each single man is to become happier, this being the true purpose of existence, while Bentam underlines that the common effort of every man is happiness.[71]

Aristotle adds that happiness is the activity of the soul in accordance with virtue, and will consist in the action of the highest part of the soul (theoretic and contemplative).[72]

Nevertheless, the principal correlates of happiness vary as one proceeds through family life.[73] In addition, experiences that contribute to happiness are a high degree of social interactions and participation in the environment: seeing friends and relatives, and belonging to organized groups (e.g., church meetings, etc.).[74] Rahner adds that we become happier when we become unselfish, this way we find love when giving love, and grow to be rich in giving.[75] According to Russell, unhappiness seems very largely due to mistaken views of the world, wrong ethics, and defective habits of life.[76] Russell also distinguishes "the sinner" as the man who is absorbed in the consciousness of the sin: he has an image of himself as he thinks he ought to be, which is in continuous conflict with his knowledge of himself as he is; on the other hand, the "narcissist" has the habit to admire oneself and wishes to be admired but will never be happy because human instinct is never and completely self-centered.[77]

When we feel deflated and discouraged by others' anger and lack of interest in ourselves, we question our own abilities: our confidence has been destroyed. In a society that is preoccupied with self-love, the emotional needs of others are frequently ignored and confidence in us would decrease accordingly. For example, many adults live with negative self-images that were acquired during childhood through the indifference or harshness of their parents. The resulting self-doubt and lack of self-confidence impairs success throughout life. In fact, confidence is characterized by an appreciation of the value and worth of the self in affiliation with any other human being. According to some Authors, severe lacks of this quality can produce depression because approval and recognition from others is one of the greatest motivators known to man.[78] In fact, "Anxiety of a man causes depression, but a good word makes it glad" (Prov. 12: 25).

4.3. EXISTENTIAL ANXIETY AND SPIRITUALITY

Life is a constant
challenge to our spiritual state,
while death and dying
are constant threats to our
spiritual balance.

There are several studies on the association between religion and the fear of death. By using the Death Anxiety Scale, Templer found that a deep involvement in religion and religious practice was linked to a lower death anxiety. In addition, for the counselor, it is important to be willing to share his/her values systems, to lower his/her religious prejudices, and to understand the religious values of the patients.[79]

Several psychotherapeutic techniques exist for facing, for reducing, or for eliminating anxiety. However, a strategy that always works is the real understanding of the characteristics of this phenomenon and why it manifests. Classically, according to the manual of psychiatry Kaplan and Sadock "anxiety is an answer to a threat that is unknown, vague, or conflicting".[80] Practically, to well see, we all are exposed, even if only mentally, to threats to our life that we do not know where they will come from. In addition, the more we perceive ourselves as vulnerable, fragile, and unprepared or not sustained by others, the more intense our anxiety and, accordingly, the somatic symptoms that characterize it. In other words, anxiety is our existential answer to the perception of a world where we do not experience spirituality, religion, and solidarity. Thus, spirituality and religion will allow us to perceive internal and external resources to combat existential anxiety. Then, the learning of whatever technique to reduce anxiety is truly the knowledge of a different philosophy of life and self-management. Practically, if we perform exercises of relaxation, of autogenic training, and of respiration (always suggested for reducing anxiety) without, contemporarily, philosophically, and spiritually restructuring our life, then anxiety can be reduced, at times can disappear, but it will reappear shortly after because we have not changed inside.

This double psycho-spiritual intervention was in the mind of the first theorists of the techniques of relaxation for anxiety (classically autogenic and yoga training). In fact, the exercises of relaxation, were accompanied by mental formulas based on life, as "the formulas of indifference" ("I feel calm and happy, my problems are indifferent to me"), and of spirituality ("I feel connected to the others. I perceive a universal solidarity that clears me") etc.

Subsequently, the deep religious, spiritual, and existential meaning of relaxation techniques were lost, remaining only what we know as practices for "reducing the anxiety". It will be to us to historically return to the origin of our life and to restructure our job, our family life, and, why not?, our project of life to remain always to the rudder of our existence. Other techniques better known as cognitive-behavioral techniques, aim to change those ideas or mental formulas that we tell us to make us anxious, for example: "I will never make it. It is about to happen me something. Anything I do at the end of it the world collapses on me". It is always the usual point. In addition, the spiteful little words that we tell to us "to fill us with fear and to make our heart palpitate" represent our model of life, and therefore, the way according to which we have spiritually and psychically structured our life.

Why then, not to try to convince us that "The world has a place for me and everybody is happy that I exist"!? A great thought and a great acquisition! Anxiety is there always: to think or not to have a place in the world, to believe or not in the help and solidarity of the others, to perceive or not affection and love of the people who are near. Moreover, these value systems also create the core themes of spirituality.

Usually spirituality is defined by some Authors as the "transcendent quest for meaning and happiness; an integrative energy".[81] Cross-cultural studies about spirituality found four elements common in the discourses about spirituality:[82]

1.   *Connectedness*: considered as the feeling a person has to be emotionally linked to self, others, nature and deity.

2.   *Meaning*: as being at the center of the personal quest of each human being.

3.   *Transcendence*: that is, feeling to be connected to a transcendence dimension.

4.   *Values and beliefs*: it is indicated that there is a "congruence of values and beliefs with feelings and behavior".[83]

"Spirituality, from the Latin word 'spiritus', breath, is a fundamental orientation to one's life and to the ground of all life; it is the source of one's posture towards living, and the nature of one's connection to all things, and of one's perception of an ultimate reality. One's spirituality engenders a way of being and experiencing, involving meaning, wholeness, openness to infinite, and connectedness to others and the natural world" (Kutz, 1999; ASERVIC White Paper, 1997 in Oliver J. Morgan, 2007)[84].

Table 4 – Existential anxiety and spirituality. Spirituality can be considered a way that each human being uses to overcome the own existential anxiety, and whatever links the own existence to the fear of being hopelessness and helplessness.

Domain	Fear	Spiritual Force
Existence	Hopelessness	Infusion of hope
Interpersonal	Isolation	Connection
Resilience	Helplessness	Feeling assisted by a superior Entity or from prayer
Anonymity	Feeling worthless and without a value and scope in the own life	Feeling to have a value and a place in the world
Weakness	Feeling psychologically/ emotionally vulnerable and chronically needy of assistance	Feeling psychologically/ emotionally strong and helpful towards the others
Family	Being without family; feeling that family is not accepting	Feeling with a nourishing family; feeling a member of a loving and accepting family; feeling a member of an extended family
Intelligence	Feeling without ideas and knowledge to master the world	Using the spiritual intelligence and religion to interpret the world
Priorities	Confusion about priorities during existential choices	A clear program of priorities in the own life
Education	Using learning and school to compete in life	Using learning and school to acquire deeper understanding of self and others

Figure 15 – The transaction from counseling to spiritual counseling requires a change in focus, starting from being centered on techniques to being centered on attitudes, and vice versa. The discourse on spiritual counseling is comprehensive of specific qualities of the counselors. However, those people who are already involved in spiritual/religious counseling need to focus on specific practical strategies in order to lower the intuitive part and to strengthen the pragmatic approach.

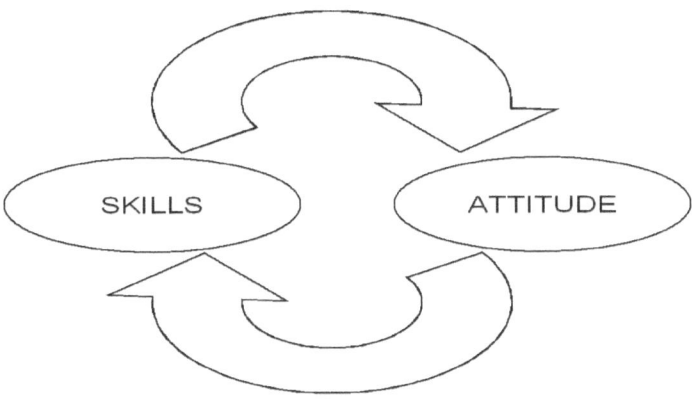

Figure 16 – Spirituality is a sort of filter for "softness" that transforms behaviors, feelings, and emotions.

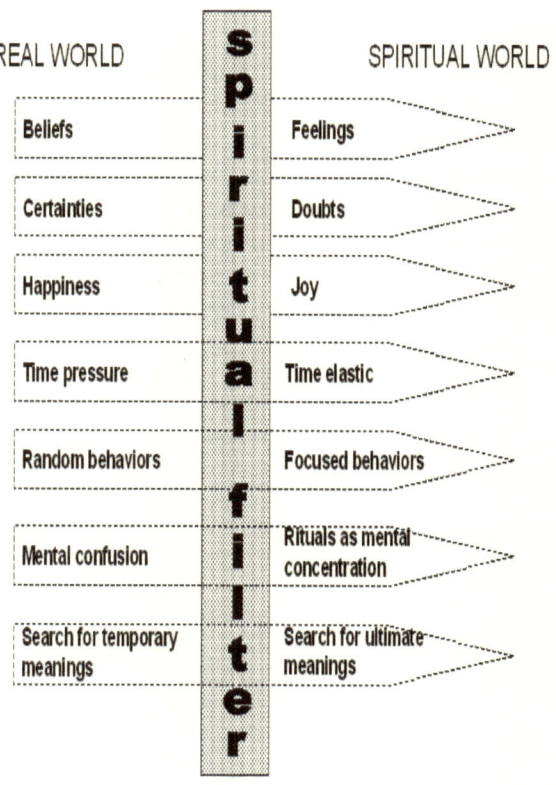

Spirituality is a "soft" transformation of values, emotions, beliefs, and behaviors,

4.4. BUILDING A TASK FORCE FOR SPIRITUAL COUNSELING

In spiritual counseling,
feelings of connectedness
shall prevail also amongst
spiritual workers.

A Unit for Spiritual Counseling (USC) is created by a team of people who use their own ability for relationship with distressed people to reduce the affliction in a person who is victim of an accident, disaster, natural calamity, war, or illnesses. Apart from this, people working in a team for spiritual counseling share, in equal amount, strategies and attitudes, aware that these are mutually influencing the approach to a sick person. Besides, the action of people who operate in the USC is characterized by the existence of standardized interventions, predetermined, and characteristic for every specific client: victims of disasters, robberies, violence, emotional crisis, illness, etc. Moreover, clients, since victims of a stressful life event, hold an acute emotional distress, sometimes limited for duration and related to the type of psychic and physical trauma causing their grief. Basically, also in the most preoccupying conditions, there are several stages or "theatres" where a counselor can apply the own strategies: i) soon before or after a diagnosis of a serious illness; ii) some days or weeks before a preoccupying diagnosis; iii) few days after a diagnosis; iv) during hospitalization; v) during admissions to hospital. Throughout these moments, a counselor can find a particular affective resonance with one of more of these "scenarios" or events, according to his or her own emotional predisposition. In fact, some helpers prefer the period of hospital admission. Others rather like to stay close to patients when they are hospitalized or when a worrying diagnosis is delivered.

Therefore, the team work for spiritual counseling might be created by people who come from a variety of fields of social works or not, and that have as own goal that to offer their own spiritual support to people who are victims of an existential loss: victims of accidents or disasters, people with acute emotional reactions to an important event, victims of catastrophes or natural calamity, victims of wars, people in state of poverty or indigence, children oppressed by abuses and violence from adults, persons persecuted by physical and psychic violence, and finally, people with an illness. In a certain sense, there could be a sort of direct connection between the personal and historical experience that a counselor receives, and his/her attitude and inclination to spiritual counseling (Fig. 17). In fact, since spiritual counseling is also a technical transformation of a personal and existential experience –in a certain sense, a familiarity with some problem transformed in counseling skills–, then we can find a lot of intuitive people working in these teams, showing a natural inclination to empathy. Thus, this progressive acquisition of specific spiritual strategies will perfection an ongoing process of personal growth of each counselor, and will "assemble" pieces of his/her personal experiences into practical skills to be employed during the assistance of distressed people. In addition, for a series of spontaneous and emotional affinities, counselors working in a team will go through a process of self-selection, each one choosing to address his/her own attention to a typology of patients, rather than to another, since s/he feels to share, or to understand, the emotional reactions of those clients that make his/her target. Furthermore, occasionally for one personal history of theirs, helpers feel affectively closer to a type of client rather than another one, since they themselves had direct or indirect experience of some typologies of trauma now affecting their clients. For example: helpers that help terminal patients because they had a relative with a similar illness.

Whatever is the reason for choosing to work with some typologies of clients, each helper refers to the own ability and force to interact with people who need a committed counseling. Furthermore, the same helpers and health personnel operating in counseling, make important existential choices regarding their own motivation, and the values to which they draw in order to offer their own support to needy people suffering from a particular existential condition, momentary and recent, or chronic and progressive. For these reasons, the team of spiritual counselors is tied up to a hospital plan that makes them operational and based on the possibility of: i) rapid evaluations of the presenting problem; ii) dedicated interventions for any kind of problem; iii) the possibility of fast and effective counseling wherever and whenever it is needed.

In short, the strategy of intervention of a USC is frequently represented by the *strategic counseling*, namely a relationship between an operator and a distressed person who is characterized by the use of communicative, psycho-spiritual, and interpersonal techniques, sometimes limited to the time tightly necessary for overcoming the presenting grief. Other times, spiritual counseling is focus-centered like other brief psychotherapies, and comprises supporting interventions limited to specific problems that have been reported by patients in hospital: e.g., fear of the hospital, concern for the diagnosis, stress for the therapy, depression after hospitalization, etc. Although these problems are focused, the whole package of intervention can last longer, depending on the therapeutic contract between counselors and clients. Other times, several counselors can rotate to support the same patient. Besides, nothing is left to improvisation. In fact, the counselors in the USC usually articulate the one with the other during their operations. Basically, each helper behaves in a coordinated and predestined manner on a known problem, with predictable emotional reactions, and through several psychotherapeutic and spiritual strategies already experimented and specific for that kind of client.

Usually, the existence of specific standardized interventions, and a shared strategy for spiritual counseling, will allow a better use of time, efforts, and will avoid undesired emotional reactions in the counseled clients. Thus, as the spiritual strategies become more and more refined, we can get a model which is more or less standardized, repeatable, and time sparing. This will consent greater efficiency and effectiveness. Basically, *the client of spiritual counseling is a person who presents with a condition of particular psychic stress, characterized by an intense emotional reaction tied up to an identifiable factor (accident, violence, a relative's death, the own illness, theft, earthquake, etc.) suggesting that a standard consolatory intervention will get scarce effects.* Consequently, due to the specificity and the dynamic articulation of the actions of a team of spiritual counseling, then a high-speed identification of the needs of each patient is possible, together with a rapid diagnosis of his/her probable emotional reactions to the moment: anger, terror, anxiety, depression, etc. Moreover, the existence of specific existential skills, will allow to spiritual counselors a prompt assessment of the risk that clients have to self-injure, and of the typology and gravity of their existential problems: for example if grief or feelings of gilt are expected or pathological. Essentially, these processes of selection help a counselor, with a specific spiritual training, in a prudent judgment on the own actions by reducing to the least one the risk of hazardous and unrehearsed interventions of counseling, or an overload of job for the application of techniques and answers of which s/he is not totally sure.

Figure 17 – Spiritual counselors can be sharing many things in common with clients, for example a personal history, that partly or totally resembles that of their clients. This rich experience summed up to the acquisition of specific counseling skills, promotes a better understanding of clients' needs. In addition, both helpers and clients might have developed a specific spiritual inclination born from similar histories of past experiences. Finally, all this, should increase the insight of each therapist and his/her empathy.

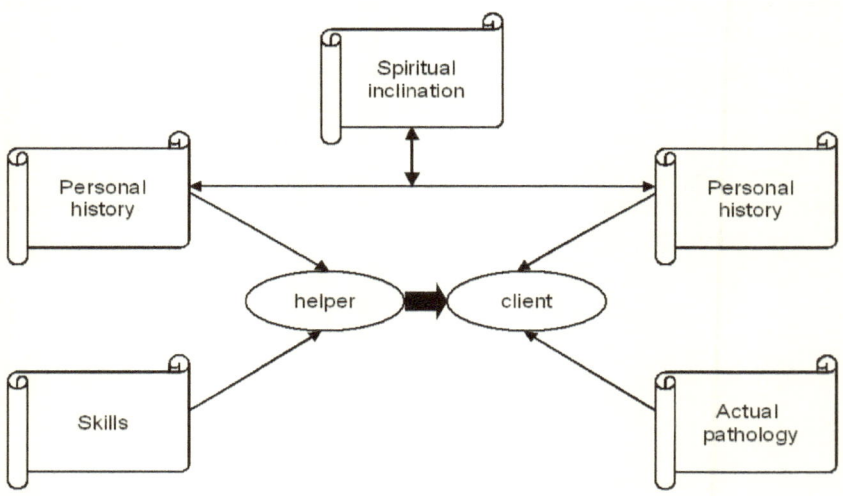

A variety of specialists, each one with a different background, can thus become spiritual helpers, all united by the fact that in their intervention, emphasis is furnished to different interpersonal skills: to the relationship and the communication (as in the standard helping), to the mutual liking (as in the relationship among friends), to the empathy (as in psychotherapeutic relationships), to the mutual walk (as in spiritual helping), to the care of the body (as in medical care), to the promotion of the feeling of connection between self and others (as in spiritual counseling), to the strengthening of the knowledge about the self (as in the therapies based on insight), to the pardon of the self (as in religious therapy), to the search of a new meaning in life (as in the logotherapy of Victor Franckl).

Besides, always in view of the standard articulation of the client-centered spiritual therapy, apart from the personal inclinations and skills, the objectives of the helper have to be clear, specific, transmissible from an operator to the other, and modifiable only through a sharing with other people of the team of the structure in which the helper operates. Thus, a coordination in the actions of spiritual counseling, besides accelerating the procedures of every helper, also allows a reduction in the duration of the therapy, and in the risk of surprises and chaos that almost always rise from helpers that are forced "to invent what to do and to tell in a certain occasion". Besides, the articulation and the standardization of the spiritual counseling in hospital also characterize the operators. For example, there are counselors specialized in the diagnosis of a pathology, and counselors that spend most of their time bedside in oncology or AIDS centers. This subsequent specialization would increase the client's trust in the hospital and health center, and would facilitate a higher degree of receptivity of the health operator in the treated pathologies and related existential issues.

As some Authors suggest, a spiritual counselor shall be in contact with all religious representatives of the local community. In fact, Prof. Franck C. Budd, of the United States Air Force, gives clear indications to spiritual counselors:[85]

1. The spiritual counselor shall know the local clergy in the area where s/he operates, by visiting them or giving a speech in the community where the believers meet.

2. The spiritual counselor shall welcome as a resource the role of the religious representative. As many of them have not time to turn to spiritual counseling, by knowing that a counselor has no intention to persuade the believers to accept another faith, the local clergy can help in soothing disputes or cases of religious intemperance.

3. The local clergy can carry a valuable experience in spiritual counseling during crises and other life troubles. They may be glad

to share these experiences with people (counselors) working in the local health system.

4.   The spiritual counselor shall always keep in touch with the local clergy in order to share information and experiences, and to build a collaborative and supporting community network for some patients.

5.   The spiritual counselor should remember that many clergy hold master and doctoral degree in counseling, and their experience shall be considered by spiritual counselors as a resource and an opportunity to learn from people who have a special familiarity with community problems.

6.   The spiritual counselor shall always be respectful of the patients' and community clergy and religion, and a particular attention should be kept in avoiding tactless comments or phrases about religion, faith, and clergy.

7.   Finally, a spiritual counselor shall be able to create a network of collaboration with local religious leaders, pastors, clergy, etc., since these people hold particular skills in solving matters related to the resolution of guilt, finding meaning in life, dealing with death and loss, forgiveness, and the role of commitment in relationships.

Figure 18 – Teamwork in spiritual counseling is a dominant aspect for delivering to clients the idea that there is agreement and alliance amongst the people who counsel them. Without this embedded idea of work alliance, clients lose the feeling that their primary caregivers are also mirrors of their family members. In other words, the team should act and participate as a family nucleus during the interaction with clients and patients. In a traditional counseling setting, this is not central, and each helper acts often independently on the same client with whom other helpers are operating.

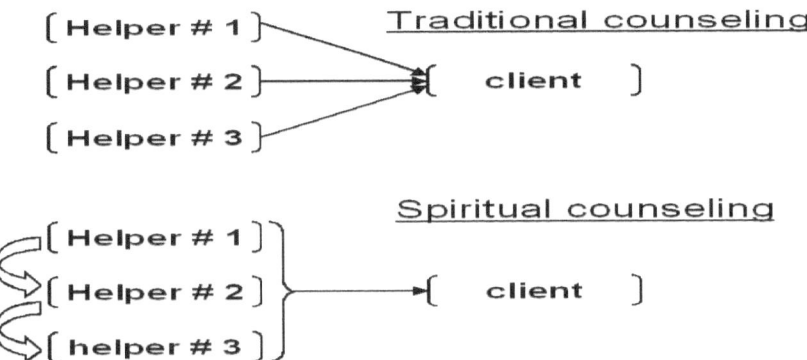

Figure 19 – Dyad helper's/client's complexity. During the passage of time, with the progression of the illness, a client reaches a higher degree in his/her spiritual development. At the same time, a counselor is helped by client's growth, and, consequently, reduces the own personal efforts to counsel. As time passes, a counselor is helped by the increased autonomy of clients in insights and independent growth.

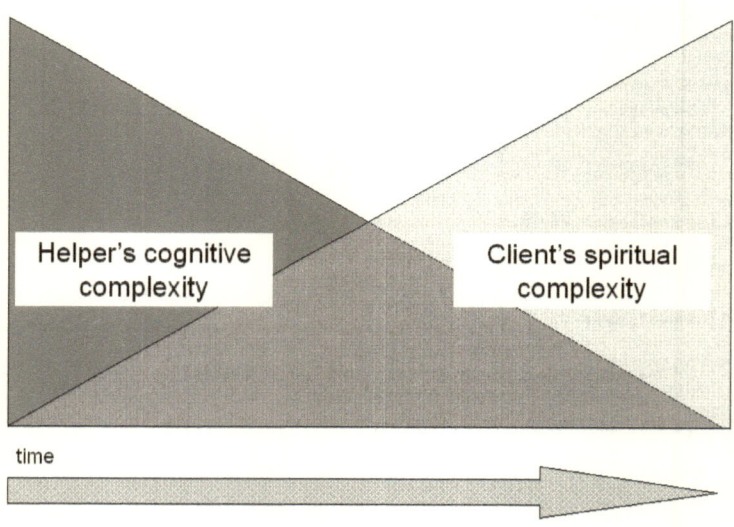

4.5. THE PROPER SETTING FOR SPIRITUAL COUNSELING

A spiritual atmosphere
is like a basket of flowers
delivering benefits to the lone souls.

Spiritual counseling cannot take place "anywhere". Apart from the real requirements of the hospital, it is up to spiritual counselors to regulate the setting to infuse to clients the idea of the "holiness of that meeting". In open spaces, or outside the hospital, it is easier to create proper spaces for this specific counseling. Even a Temple, a Church, a Parish, a Synagogue, a Community Center can serve for the goal. But inside a hospital, things become more complicated. Like in any psychotherapy, the setting is considered fundamental for any therapeutic relationship. Besides, not any location is ethically acceptable for starting a psychotherapeutic session. Even more peculiar is the setting for spiritual counseling. Besides, in hospital it is important to contain an innate attitude to do "everything everywhere". This is a common scenario in many precarious health systems. For example, in problematic hospitals, the right for privacy of a client is constantly abandoned. Basically, each counselor shall feel comfortable with the setting, since basic spiritual strategies contemplate concentration and silence as central therapeutic moments for care. Also a patient shall feel to openly express the own anguish and pain, but also to close in him/herself if s/he prefers. Sometimes, some locals of the chapel in the hospital, or a place for nondenominational worship, can serve to the purpose. Another important reason to choose with care the setting is given by the fact that it certifies and confirms the qualities of the helper by giving him/her (greater) credibility. In fact, if a counselor chooses to speak of the afterlife into a crowded place and full of disorder, what s/he will say will not be believed. If, in the moment of stress and peak spirituality of a client, a telephone rings, the whole counseling session will be worthless. Then a particular care is needed both of the places and of the furnishings.

The underlying theoretical framework for the selection of a proper setting, usually resides in the idea that we are able to appreciate cognitively many stimuli in our life as carrying some degree of embedded spirituality, although there is no guiding element to make this statement completely true or false. In religion, symbols often ease the process of understanding and identification with complex concepts. In addition, symbols have served to the purpose to guiding people to fast identification of some religious movements.

Thus, the religious iconography with the mass of religious paintings full of symbolism has paralleled all religious movements to the point that, nowadays, it is almost impossible to separate religion from pictorial symbols, given the mutual interdependence. Practically, figures associated to colors, and a specific "religious atmosphere" all bear a tremendous impact on the human psych and on the understanding of some central concepts in major religions. Then, for what concerns the application of these concepts to hospitals and to the health system, we learn that it is important to construct a proper environment for hosting people, sick people or underprivileged persons, by offering them a *spiritual environment* which shall not be shocking, and that shall be apt to carry a meaning in a multi-denominational health center. Putting a Cross on a wall has a meaning for people who are Christians but there are many others that profess other creeds. Other symbols are then needed and shall be identified. Much more interesting is the opportunity to create an environment that carries the same spiritual impact for each person independently from religious faith. Again, spirituality and religion shall find independent routes of self-expression. Therefore, the creation of a *spiritual environment*, not solely as a place where to pray, is a goal of spiritually oriented health centers.

4.6. STANDARDIZED INTERVENTIONS

Spiritual counseling
is achieved by
a friendly approach in
a spirit of brotherhood
with colleagues.

When spiritual counselors work in a team, they acquire the same trainings when in relationship with the same category of clients. This allows an easier and more effective application of counseling strategies. This, to every way, nothing removes from the autonomy of the intervention of a counselor who, according to his/her own knowledge and personal character, chooses from a list of options of programmed interventions to which s/he has, however, been prepared. This way, "as from manual", a spiritual counselor will select what style of relationship and communication is more opportune with a category of patients. Moreover, the spirit of collaboration amongst the components of the spiritual team is a valuable instrument of self-help to reduce the workload, and the natural stress of working with people with serious illnesses. In addition, a team of spiritual counseling also reduces the stress and the workload of other health specialists.

Almost always, the helpers and the spiritual counselors in a hospital are the specialists that more frequently stay closer to patients. At the same time, the reduction of patient's distress is a catalyst to a better evolution of an illness, also because a psychic pain is often the condition of debut of more important and lasting physical problems. In addition, a spiritual counselor is also a person who starts to take in charge a patient who, for the first time, is experiencing progressive shocks and losses. Only subsequently, other specialists will take in charge that patient for more specific and prolonged treatments. Until then, a spiritual counselor is the only referent for help that people have available for coping with extraordinary, important, unexpected, and terrible events. However, as the helper is a person endowed with one professionalism of his/her, s/he will have to learn not to be exploited by other specialists. These last, by not having any aspiration to interact with distressed patients, might allege as motivation for deserting a spiritual approach the fact that "patients' emotions are not their stuff". This is evident both in devoted environments as hospitals, jails, community, and in more specific moments like during the help to people victims of violence and abuse. Theoretically, whoever should professionally be ready to take care of a suffering patient, and spiritual counseling really is relevant for a physician, a nurse, a police officer, or simply a volunteer. However, this is not always possible and the "official" spiritual counselor soon has to make clear when, with whom, and how s/he will intervene if third parties ask for his/her help.

Other times, this trial is easier when a team of spiritual counselors is legally constituted, a denomination is given, and decides to operate side by side to some stable organisms like the Police, the Red Cross, the street Unities, the prison guards, the nurses of a hospital. Thus, a preventive agreement between the personnel of the spiritual team and the organs asking for its support are important to avoid incomprehension or confusions in roles and in tasks. Done this, it will be important to appraise other variables that favor or hamper the job of a team or a spiritual counselor. One of these aspects can be defined as *factor Kappa* that establishes if the target on which the intervention of spiritual counseling is directed, is correct, or if the counselor is losing his/her precious time for a cure that is up to other specialists.

Kappa is a ratio given by the following value:

$$Kappa = True\ Positives\ /\ False\ Positives$$

Indicating with "True positives" those patients that indeed can take advantage of the spiritual counseling, and that can be suitable as a true target. On the other hand, with "False positives" we intend those patients and clients that have been reported to a spiritual counselor, but only for mistake, for a scarce selection, or simply "to relieve the load of some specialists that should follow them instead". The risk that a spiritual counselor turns instead into a basket where to transfer "uncomfortable patients" or those that "bother" to other specialists, is always high.

For this reason, *Kappa* can assume different values and meanings:

- If the value of *Kappa is greater or equal to 1* it means that a counselor works well, that clients have been properly selected, and that almost all the people reported to a counselor are, indeed, people needing psychological assistance and spiritual help.

- If the value of *Kappa is inferior to 1*, it means that there are many "false positive" clients, and that not all the patients, in reality the majority, reported to a spiritual counselor are true targets. Perhaps, other health specialists are using a spiritual counselor as a "basket for other problems".

In conclusion, it is important to establish immediately who needs spiritual counseling and who, indeed, does not need it. This avoids an overload of job that exceeds the real requirements and helps a spiritual counselor to spare emotional resources and time to devote all himself/herself to a person really afflicted. If Kappa is always inferior to one, that is, if false positives or false alarms exceed the number of patients that really need spiritual counseling, then we reach the burnout of the resources of a counselor and his/her immediate impasse. In this instance, a spiritual counselor perceives that s/he has no longer the support from colleagues and medical staff. At the same time, the same counselor understands that s/he is called to intervene only for soothing minds and conflicts that little have to deal with the demands of a spiritual assistance. Accordingly, a counselor will run into a progressive loss of interest, and into a reduction in the quality of his/her own intervention. For these reasons, it is of vital importance to reach a mutual understanding and agreement between medical staff and spiritual counselors. In fact, this strategy requires from counselors a profound concentration, humanity, and serenity to deliver an effective and decisive therapy.

4.7. THE SPECTER OF A DISEASE

Nothing draws a man
nearer to spirituality
than death and dying.

When a person gets a serious illness, the own body and the own spirit slowly surrender their territories, their sure beaches, to the progression of an illness. This is usually defined as "loss", and it indicates our separation from where we had invested our vital energy. According to the psychological theory of the "object relations" a person's bond with animate "objects" (example, other people, family, etc.) or inanimate objects (e.g., his/her own job, his/her own social position) is tied up to pleasant feelings and a sense of inner gratification. Instead, the separation from the same objects produces disagreeable feelings, depression, anxiety, and the perception that life is fading away. We reassume for clarity: during life a person emotionally forms "object relations", that is, forms emotional links with other people, with himself, included his/her own body, or with inanimate but important objects like job, social safety, etc. Instead, during a serious illness, still before a patient reaches the advanced stages, a series of crises or anticipatory "mourning" occurs in him

We can thus find, in a terminal patient, apart form a *sense of loss of the own physical integrity*, also the anxiety for the absence of a social role or the anxiety for becoming a "burden" inside the own family. In effects, these are central in the depression during illnesses, and the loss of hope (hopelessness), and of the possibility to be helped (helplessness), are added because of a real poor health. Furthermore, amongst the events that worry a lot a sick person, one is very important. It is the fear to lose one's own neuromuscular autonomy or, more exactly, the use of the own body and of visceral functions as symbols of the loss in self-sufficiency. Amongst the other central losses, we find the *fear to lose the control of the self* as prediction of deficits in the superior cerebral functions. Consequently, before the real development of any neuronal deficit, a patient is scared about becoming unable to make a congruous reality test: this is better known as the worry of "becoming crazy". Other losses happen to the level of image, not only physical, but also social. For example, many patients are worried about how they will appear to the eyes of other people. A sick person, thus, is concerned about any "evident sign" of the own illness, and whether or not s/he could appear "strange" or "unattractive" to others. Consequently, those who want to conceal their health, are concerned about any unsolicited enquires starting from friends or family. We can name this as *fear of the loss in the social image*.

Other ill people are worried about secondary effects of the own pathology on the skin. In fact, the skin and the mucous membrane can become the "façade" of what happens inside the body: dermatitis, mycoses, herpetic infections, sarcoma of Kaposi (in AIDS), and hair loss during anti-cancer therapies. In addition, a simple and innocent furuncle can, instead, instigate intense emotional reactions in those who live their own body as unpredictable, or, at least, insecure refuge of the organic events that take part in it. Thus, the terror of a real or only imaginary deformity can afflict whatever sick person. Consequently, because of these fears, a patient creates a series of relevant rituals to oppose the lived threat of decay in the own image. For example, a greater attention is given to health behaviors. Someone can start special diets. Other times, small make-ups are found "to disguise" the progression of the illness. Other patients develop an intolerable perception of tiredness in "having to put on a mask" every time that are together with the others. Usually, they try to conceal their own pain and mortifications under an impassive face, if not, even, serene. We can name all these concerns as *fear of deformity*.

Nonetheless, when the illness progresses, the feeling of control of the own body as a means of social relationship, of locomotion, of perception, and of independence from the others can be lost. Moreover, a physical debility, a generalized discomfort, depression, and pessimism can reduce, in a worrisome way, the ability of a patient to manage in a brave way the relationships with the family, the friends, and the others. Basically, a patient is afraid that the progressive isolation determined by hospitalization and therapies usually reduces the own social life, and might lead to the abandonment by the own friends, or an overload of job in the own family. Social anxiety is intense in those who have held concealed their illness that they believed "embarrassing" (for example, AIDS; mastectomy, etc.). Practically we here are dealing with a *fear of social isolation*.

The loss of friends, even if only imaginary, and therefore, the possibility to be unable to receive the solidarity and the affection of people because of the distance, of the impossibility to meet them, of the frequent hospitalizations, all can cause an insecurity during social interactions and an anxiety for not being able to program meetings and moments of sharing with the dearest ones. All this intensifies the depression and the social isolation in a patient, adding unwanted restrictions to the heavy limitations already created by a disease. To this, a sense of discouragement is summed up for not being able to inform the own friends and often the own relatives of one's own illness. Besides, the "fatigue" determined by therapies, muscular weakness, and continuous hospitalizations can also restrict in a sick person the execution in the lighter jobs. The consequence is a threat to the sense of self-autonomy and to the engagement in the activities of the own family. We can describe these concerns as *loss of social solidarity and self-autonomy*.

Besides, in all the chronic illnesses, a fear always exists of losing the control of one's own daily activities, and this anguish intensifies when such control is indeed reduced. As a result, the self-esteem of the sick person lowers because s/he fears that, because of the illness, s/he will lose the ability to work in self-sufficient and independent ways. In consequence of this, a sick person is afraid of not getting a series of gratifications: for example to take a walk, to be with other people, to travel, or to go to meet friends. Finally, we meet the fear of death and dying. Then, we come across the fear to lose the control of the self as biological, psychological, and spiritual being. Thus, we understand why many patients are afraid of "becoming crazy" and "losing their head" even before being really bad.

In the patients who are more spiritually oriented, the fear to die is, instead, tied up to the fear to die alone, in complete anonymity, out of the social context of a group where everyone lives with the others (aggregative dimension), for the others (altruistic dimension), and in the others (historical or commemorative dimension). For example, AIDS is lived as "illness to be hidden". Thus, the death for AIDS is anticipated, in the mind of patients and their families as a threat to the loss in the image and social credibility. Consequently, truth will be hardly covered to friends and relatives when parents will have to explain them the reasons of such "premature and unexpected death". Therefore, in many illnesses, silence and anonymity often deprive a patient of the possibility to be consoled, loved, and sustained really from the dearest people. Accordingly, a spiritual counselor will have to fill many voids of a patient, and usually, in his/her action of love and counseling, s/he will often replace, for a patient, also its darlings, the nearest people, and even friends.

4.8. DEATH AND DYING IN LITERATURE

Spiritual courage
infuses each human being
with unexpected strength
during unpredictable events.

The book *Death of Ivan Il'ic* of Tolstoy[86], represents one of the most beautiful literary accounts on the suffering and the feelings of a man who faces the last days of his life. At the center of the tale, we do not find only a man who fights with desperation against his terminal illness, but also a human being that rediscovers with bitterness the lie and the indifference of those people who live around him, above all his relatives. The stages described for the emotional reactions to the diagnosis of his serious illness are the classical ones, found in who lives under the same conditions of Ivan Il'ic. This way, in the narration of Ivan, we find the first impact with the difficulty of the physician in talking in clear terms to a patient. Thus, a family doctor, then as today, can be unprepared to face the anguish of the very ill person, above all, when a patient needs clear information. Moreover, the emotional obstacle in a physician often intensifies the fears of a patient who would have the right to set all the questions to understand what is happening in his/her own body.

Basically, the effort of a patient, as that of Ivan, is "to translate in a clear language a *doctor's* (my italics) nebulous and ruffled technical terms, with the purpose to be able to read an answer to his/her (patient's) interrogation: 'Am I bad, very bad or the things don't go then so badly?'".[87] A person with a serious illness also gains a particular sensibility towards other sick people, and partly he considers himself similar to them. He lives as if an invisible but strong bond somehow united the destinies of all the people who suffer, or that are ill, to his. Thus, s/he suffers and rejoices with whom s/he considers similar to the self. Moreover, s/he is worried about the clinical evolution of the pathology in people with the same illness. This process of identification is inevitable in people with the same pathology, and it can represent an obstacle to their own psychological comfort. In fact, this attitude to comparison is more pervasive when a patient associates himself to people who have the advanced stages of the same illness. The same happens to Ivan Il'ic: "If someone spoke to his presence of a patient, of a dead person, or of a patient happily re-established, he soon straightened the ears hiding the emotion, setting questions, and drawing conclusions, above all when the illness seemed analogous to his".[88]

Other times also the search of alternative therapies is frequent. Such a need to try some cures that are different from those offered by the own physician or hospital is always present. Perhaps it represents not so much the desire of a best cure, but rather, the need not to surrender in front of what seems inevitable or not to kill the hope. At times, also the alternative remedy, once proven vain, also reduces the hope to improve: "A homeopath duly consulted totally offered a different diagnosis and recommended a medicine that Ivan Il'ic took for eight days".[89] Other patients complain about the treatments received in some medical structures, and feel sorry for not understanding a science that strives to be exact but that, often, results incomprehensible for a lot of people, since it is expresses itself with what Tolstoj defines "nebulous technical terms".[90] Continuing the progression of the illness, we find that the sick person can also come to personalize his/her own pain, as it happens to Ivan Il'ic that calls it with "him".[91]

As a result, the constant proximity between a man and his/her physical pain, at the beginning is still attenuated by the bearable characteristics of the own anguish, so that this person is still able to become distracted from it and to treat it as an extraneous physical fact to his/her Self. However, as pain and suffering increase, such separation becomes less and less evident to the point that pain itself is now personified and becomes a quality of the Self, and prevails on it at the same time. This means that when a patient refers to him/herself, s/he usually does it only by speaking about his/her own pain with which s/he identifies. This is a struggle that is not easily resolved. We shall then considerer that in these instances, a *pain "is in" the person and that pain "is" the person.* The constancy of pain, the impossibility for a patient to be free of it at least for once, the time spent to listen the imperceptible changes of its intensity, its deaf and spiteful constancy and obstinacy, inevitably lead a person to attribute a spirit to the own pain and therefore a proper wish. The same happens to Ivan Il'ic who faces his own pain as if it were a person: "*He* [pain] didn't call him [Ivan Il'ic] to make an action complete, an act, but only because he [Ivan] looked straight at *him* [pain] in the eyes and he atrociously suffered. [...] The side hurt him: *he* [pain] was there, he [Ivan] could not forget it".[92]

The family that surrounded Ivan Il'ic did not seem to give a lot of weight to his conditions. Or it did not perhaps want because it is always arduous, for the one who lives next to a dying person, to take the correct emotional distances "to avoid" to remain, also it, emotionally involved. An accomplice of this attitude can be the slowness of an illness. The natural consequence is that things often seem not to change. Besides, who is around a patient could not realize what happens to the afflicted one if s/he misses a complete verification of what a sick person is silently suffering. In the history of Ivan Il'ic, a difficult family situation is added, but not so much. A thin alliance amongst the other relatives had created a "curtain of silence" so that the collective peaceful life was not upset. In addition, the description that Tolstoj leaves us about the character during the terminal moments of his illness is clear and easily comparable with similar experiences. For example, the attitude of self-analysis and listening of the body that from being a friend becomes hostile and therefore unpredictable. Thus, a body with eccentric and unknown humors, however, not anymore an ally of life for a person but, clearly, a capricious and deceitful enemy.

Naturally, this almost schizoid division between a man and its body is accentuated more and more when pain advances. This way, an illness takes its revenge by becoming not only a presence but also an entity conflicting inside the same person. This condition is similar to that of those people who have visual or auditory hallucinations. Here, the splitting between the person who sees the hallucinated object, and the object itself, does not allow some doubt anymore. Surely, a patient deals with something else from the self, or rather with an entity external to the body. *The illness is thus lived as something else from the self*, above all, it is lived by a patient as foolish, full-bodied in its destructivity, unexpected in its fortuity, and, therefore, undesired. The last pages of the history of Ivan Il'ic represent a unique philosophical conception about human existence. Tolstoj, through the thoughts of his character, already takes back a theme known to us. The human being who avoids questioning himself on his own existence because fear prevails. This way, a suffering patient, to deceive him/herself, mixes the meanings, and chooses the easiest theories or, to a certain extent, the way of forgetfulness, as shown in the book: "All of your existence has not been anything else other than a perennial lie, destined to disguise the questions on life and on death".[93]

Nevertheless, at the end, one slender answer also comes us from the words of Ivan Il'ic that almost astonished realizes that so much affliction that had characterized his dying (a progressive process inserted in his own existence) did not find a real correspondence with death itself. This last, finally arrived, showed a more serene face, tremendously conflicting with what had preceded it. Besides, we know that a human being only knows dying and not death, since dying sometimes, represents a physiological situation from which one can return to life. This is shown us by our manifold experiences, some of which very tragic, in which many times we have told to ourselves: "I have felt as if I were dying!". Yet, nobody has any knowledge about death. Nobody has ever come back to tell us what it was. Yet, really in the last instants of the own existence, when a person is about to exhale, s/he can enrich himself/herself with this unique and unrepeatable experience, as it also happens to Ivan Il'ic: "He looked for his past, scared in front of death, and he didn't find it anymore. Where was death?... And what was it? No terror anymore, since there was not death anymore. A big light instead of death".[94]

4.9. CHANGING VALUE SYSTEM

The destiny of all our life is to enlighten us about the meaning of the last days of our existence.

Victor Hugo too, in his book *Death Row Inmate,* reports the emotional states of a person who feels that death is near him. The debut is achieved by the use of simple words, clean, sincere, and full of regret but also of serene remembrances. This is what a person lives emotionally when s/he tells goodbye to life. It affects, above all, a goodbye to the thoughtlessness, but also the thought that was able to, and succeeded in, building plans and projects in all liberty, above all in comparison to what now constitutes, instead, an undeniable truth.[95] The same happens to the character of Victor Hugo: "It was always a party in my imagination. I could think about what I wanted, I was free".[96]

Other times our mind could be obsessed by the idea of the presence of whatever illness. Then, some people try to free themselves from this fixed image by denying the reality, or, rather, by acting as if nothing were happening. Yet, the people who defend themselves from the anguish by denying the reality (the fact to be very sick), usually walk on a route full of traps. It is enough a nil, news on TV, a small discomfort, because this ephemeral liberty is overcome by such a heavy tyranny. Basically, mind and its thoughts, and not the body that also lodges an illness, becomes imprisoned by the idea of an ongoing tragedy. The same happens in the character of Hugo: "Anything I do, it is always here, this infernal thought".[97] Thus, the difficulty in a patient often consists in succeeding in denying the evidence of the facts. Negation is an expensive defense mechanism because, in case of serious illnesses, it tries to win a reality that emerges out of all the pores. Likewise, defense mechanisms are fast and capricious when patients deal with an unexpected and undesired truth. This, above all, happens when a person has never had premonitory symptoms or risk behaviors that could make him foresee the illness of which s/he now suffers. Other daily events do not allow to a person to succeed in "forgetting" or in finding moments of peace, even if for a few minutes. Silence, loneliness, obscurity, sleep, and dreams are some conditions in which the mechanisms of negation, or the achievement of a mental relief have few possibilities to prevail. During these moments, anguish can sprout out unexpected and violent. Besides, new emotional and existential experiences of life emerge in the very sick person. It is as if s/he had on some glasses with special lenses that change dimensions, sounds, colors, and tastes of the physical and psychic reality. This can be also a moment where people become more spiritual and give a different meaning to their own existence. Some start to pray for the first time. Basically, some patients confess to see the other people through a different light, and to appreciate more extensively the "true meaning and value of things" such as friendship, solidarity, or the vacuity of what the populace seems to appraise more. Many patients also confess that not always do they succeed in sharing with the others (the so-called "healthy ones") these new meanings, very spiritual and profound. Above all, sick people look for "true values", as they confess not to appreciate anymore the "falsehood of which the society is full". As an Author writes: "In the struggle through our deepest pain and vulnerability we come to understand fully our humanity, the frail state in which we live".[98]

4.10.FACING OUR DESTINY

*When we are prisoners of
the physical world,
we escape and free ourselves
in our spiritual kingdom.*

The moments that immediately precede or follow a diagnosis of a serious illness are those in which a complete revolution of the psychological homeostasis happens in patients. These are also the instants in which a person is spiritually more vulnerable. In fact, there can be a growth of one's own religious or spiritual soul, or even a definitive departure from the own creed. In this last occurrence, a patient assumes anti-health attitudes, practically, behaviors that apparently are in opposition to those needed to maintain a relative good state of health. S/he eats more, and this way s/he does not follow a diet anymore, s/he restarts to smoke, s/he does not follow a prescribed therapy. In these occasions, a spiritual counseling can, thus, try to re-establish in a patient the attitude for self-care, or, at least, a favorable attitude towards life in general. For instance, this can be achieved by reducing, in a patient, the strong tension and anger that are physiological in these moments. It exists, to every way, a whole series of emotional reactions that begin after a diagnosis of a serious illness. Usually, the period immediately following to a diagnosis is characterized by the presence of depersonalization and derealization. In other words, a patient thinks that reality is a whole scene of a film, that other people are not real, and that, therefore, they are playing a pre-arranged role, actors of an unreal comedy. It happens also in the character of Victor Hugo immediately after the conviction to death. "Those men, those women, those children that were gathering at my passage, seemed to me some ghosts".[99]

A patient might simply feel extraneous or estranged by society, as if s/he were not part of it anymore. S/he then thinks that s/he cannot share with other people a common existential project, as s/he believes that other people are happier because knowing that they will not die "immediately". Practically, spirituality and religion are the most opportune theoretical frameworks for facing the idea of death and dying and to restore in patients the idea of a universal joy, born by sharing with other human beings the burden of solitude, isolation, and pain. This approach shall then be effective in reducing also the feeling of seclusion from a communitarian joy.

Always dealing with existential issues, we find that in all religions, the concept of death is treated as a normal topic for believers. In addition, *spirituality is a way of living without denying death.* (Christian Trappist Monks' motto is: "Memento Mortis", "Remember Your Death"). *For this reason the task of a spiritual counselor is to elaborate, together with clients (even if not ill), the idea of "life and living" without any phobic escape from the idea of death and dying.* So many people can die even before the character of Victor Hugo, a death row inmate. There are many deadly accidents, sudden deaths, unpredictable catastrophes that throw back a man into the idea of the inevitability, and daily proximity, of death. In a terminal patient, such perception of proximity is clear and strong and to this, s/he associates anguish and resignation. Yet, in who is not, or does not feel sick, this proximity is not perceived. Consequently, also the opportunity to think about a spiritual way of death and dying is not believed as a priority. In a certain way, everybody knows that s/he could immediately die, but this idea never reaches that thickness and level of awareness that it has in a person who "is sure" to die. This way the character of Victor Hugo comments: "How many people have anticipated me, young people, free and healthy, and that really counted to go to see in such day my head to fall in Place de Gréve?".[100]

In the book of Victor Hugo, there is also an indication to the sense of liberation that a person feels when, next to death, finally succeeds in speaking about his/her own anguishes, and in telling them to a friend. The character of the book will perform this miracle by writing his memorandum. In other words, he will make other people witnesses of his own sufferings that seem a shirt of strength for a free spirit. This can also be a therapeutic strategy for patients. As the character of Victor Hugo states: "However, these anguishes, the only way to suffer less of them, is observing them, besides, describing them will be a distraction for me".[101] It deals with the same effect of liberation that a patient perceives when talking of one's own anguish to a counselor, or, however, to a person who wants and "knows" how to listen. Nonetheless, in reality, we find that in people with a serious illness, there is often a difficulty to make to coincide what it appears to outsiders, that is, an apparently uninjured body, with an illness that does not show evident signs. Other times, also medical interventions are not considered a viable "solution", since they do not seem to act on the core pathology. Consequently, this throws more into discouragement those people who still hope that the therapies can end their own nightmares. The character of Hugo when talking about a doctor, comments: "[...] he also heals you from a fever, but not surely from a sentence of death!".[102]

4.11. ACCUSING THE MEDICAL STAFF, OTHERS, AND ONESELF

> *Spirituality is*
> *the harmony of our*
> *manifold identities.*

Patients in critical stages often complain with the medical personnel: "If you cannot give back to me my life why shall I take care of me?". In other words, they believe that a medical intervention that is not total and resolving, is simply palliative. The same judgment is also reserved for psychological assistance and counseling.

Honestly, this also corresponds to a common way of seeing: a physician is by some patient considered as a person who again turns a state of illness into a state of health. In other words, s/he should have the magic power to restore or to return what has gone lost. However, there are some difficulties to accept this version, since a life, above all the biological one, is rather a sequence of progressive losses. In other words, a biological existence is an addition of states of no-health in which the restoration of the normality or no-pathology is more a theoretical fact than a practical acquisition. The same process of aging, occurring during the passage of hours and minutes, represents a loss that is not curable anymore. Thus, the desire to return as before one got seriously ill, really means to attribute a miraculous power to medicine and physicians. Yet, if this is not achievable in the biological body, can be acceptable, however, for the care of the spiritual and the psychic part of a patient. For other diseases, however, it is also possible to aim to a better health and status quo, especially if there has not been an extreme decline in the health status.

Consequently, for a spiritual counselor it is crucial to weight the real expectations of clients who might invest all their hopes and attitudes to the conviction that al least with "a complete adherence to spiritual and religious rituals they can get an unexpected miracle". But, as the literature shows, "miracles" can sometimes happen, and the task of spiritual counselors is, instead, to wisely weight what clients want to achieve through adhering to spirituality, religion, prayers, etc. In fact, it is a shared idea amongst several Authors who deal with the issue of spiritual counseling, that patients' locus of control should always be internally focused. Accordingly, a naive acceptance of patient's hope to assign all the efforts, and merits of the healing, to an "external or supernatural Entity" shall be critically evaluated by spiritual counselors. A thing on which is important to work, instead, is a check of patient's life history. In effect, it is not rare to find in many patients a sour criticism of one's own past habits to which the causes of their own actual illness are attributed. This "trial to the past on today's platform", can be an impasse from which many patients do not succeed in unraveling.

Other times, these accusations are turned to other people who, rightly or wrongly, are considered the true causes of one's own actual condition. For example, this is particularly frequent in psychology where the abuse from one's own parents is the source of personality disorders or major problems. Actually, it is not the task of a spiritual counselor to favor a client in these investigations, and to peacefully accept the role of an impartial judge. Instead, during spiritual counseling, the focal point is much on "forgiving" and the motivation is on here and now. More specifically, the process of forgiving is deemed to be centered on *Self* (S), *Others* (O), and, in this case, *Life History* (LH). From this new acquisition, we expect a sort of "renovation" of patient's value system for what concerns S/O/LH, with a direct and direct effect on the appraisal process of a pathology and its consequences.

Table 5 – Reappraising Self (S), Others (O), and Life History (LH) with a focus on Forgiveness as a force in spiritual healing.

Forgiveness applied to own Self	*Forgiveness applied to the Others*	*Forgiveness applied to the own Life History*
A client reaches a new appreciation of Self, and reduces the tendency of *self-accusation* for what concerns his/her actual health status (biological or psychological).	By applying an *amnesty to others* if deemed to be responsible of one's actual health status, a client and a counselor can progress in the process of focusing and interiorization of the locus of control.	Aiming to *self-pity* is a vital target in any psychological counseling of suffering people. Past life history shall be re-examined for the "good things it teaches", also if not many positive experiences can be remembered.
A patient reconciles with his/her own body as it is, also accepting limitations and the "wounds" imposed by the actual pathology.	The patient reduces the "number" of the own enemies, real and imagined, and is ready to accept any human being, health staff, doctors, and nurses, as a resource for the own growth and spiritual enrichment. Possible episodes of medical malpractice are not impeding this progressive movement to brotherhood and sisterhood.	Past, present, and future are nicely intermingled in a meaningful whole. The own past is not accepted as an "excuse" for the present history, neither is the future acknowledged for reinforcing present attitudes to procrastinate. Clients shall not be stocked on waiting a "better medical picture before starting spiritual counseling". Spiritual counseling is for everyday life, suffering, and needs.

A patient stops blaming the self for "incorrect and past health behaviors" that lead to the present disease. A counselor solicits in a sick patient a holistic attitude to accept any part of the self and the core concept of free will. Identity is reinforced in any sector, also during imagined "faults or errors". A holistic spirituality seeks to link the "good self" with the "faulty self". Even if unhealthy behaviors conducted to present conditions, they were, anyhow, part and expression of the real self in "that moment". The Self could not have been something else.	With the help of a counselor a client accepts with a peaceful mind his "regional location in the world". This way, s/he starts to accept, full of mercy, the own city, the own country, the own "spatial collocation", even the own social and economic status if disadvantaged. "Geographical benevolence" is intended to restore an accepting attitude towards the physical conditions of the own entourage, which shall support the feeling of connectedness with neighbors. Without this compassion a patient would, instead, intensely aspire to live a "better life" in an imagined Neverland.	The "holistic spiritual being" is a mix of past and present faults and merits. Without this concept of merciful acceptance of the own biography, a risk exists for a patient to become "judge and offender" at the same time. Life history is, spiritually speaking, the ground where the self has flourished. And as humus, both acknowledged history and painful experiences are honored for a spiritual growth, self-compassion, and reconciliation.

4.12. THE MOMENT OF RECOLLECTIONS

*Spirituality helps mankind
to maintain a meaningful
thread for its multiple histories.*

In the most melancholic people, the anecdotes of their past life reappear in their minds, many times in a row. Occasionally, facts that seemed forgotten, re-emerge vivid, often bearing new favorable or sorrowful meanings. These memoirs reappear more quickly if a person feels that life is abandoning him or her. Accounts and episodes that a person thought had been cancelled, instead reappear after so many years under a different light. They usually deal with meaningful events of the own life. For example, a patient might experiences vivid faces of people met or places where s/he transited. The expression that some patient uses is: "A film of all of your life that flows in front of your eyes". *It is as if the meaning of what one lived can be extrapolated now only, in the last moments of one's own existence.* Patients, thus, reexamine the facts of their own life as if they had to look for the true value of everything that has occurred to them. The same happens at the character of Victor Hugo: "While I dream, the memoirs of my infancy and my youth appear to me one to one, sweets, calm, laughing, as in bloom islands above that vortex of black and confused thoughts that upset my brain".[103]

Usually, the situation of terminality seems to help a person to a spiritual analysis of his/her own existence. Indeed, a patient aims to the discovery of a common thread for assigning a meaning to so many fragments of an existential puzzle that, often, seems to have a proper life and an autonomous implication. As a result, the *search for a meaning* represents a constant priority in these moments, and if such meaning is met, then the worry that one's own life had not a sense will disappear.

When, instead, life is threatened by an unexpected event, like an infectious and epidemic illness (for example, a plague, leprosy, AIDS; as it usually happens in poor countries, etc.) what happens is easily verifiable in the stories narrated in the book *The Plague* by Albert Camus. Usually, an epidemic illness, for its overwhelming and immediate characteristics, finds the whole medical community, scientists, and victims unprepared and impotent to cope, scientifically and psychologically, with the precariousness of life and the facility of death. Camus narrates the history of a physician, Rieux, who starts to face in a progressive way the emergency of an explosion of plague in the town of Orano. He finds himself absorbed in the tragedies of a terminal illness, together with the victims that, clear, are delineated, with their suffering, on a background of apparent incredulity and inexplicable optimism. "Until then, sick people facilitated him in his assignment, they came to him, but for the first time the doctor felt them reticent, sheltered in the bottom of their illness with a sort of suspicious amazement".[104]

Therefore, an illness modifies the type of relationship, and the quantity of trust that a patient grants to his/her own physician. As long as a client perceives the least possibility of recovery by his/her own doctor, such interaction can always be stamped by mutual trust. However, when the same illness advances, and the curative power of a physician reduces, a person might look elsewhere for his/her own shelter, at the same time, discrediting or diminishing the effectiveness of a medical intervention. Also Camus, like other Authors, takes back the theme of time, however inevitable, whenever a man is brought to the here-and-now by his illnesses and by his pain. Actually, if the concern and the uncertainty for one's own life did not exist, a patient would always live in the present, thinking only exclusively about his own future. In other words, a man not concerned about his own life, is potentially focused on a dimension without time, containing in a sure casket the own past while submitting all of his projects, and the sense of his own existence, to the own future. On the contrary, spiritual counseling is much interested in focusing in the here-and-now, which is a way of finding resilience and strategies for facing what a man and a woman value in their present. Instead, in a person with a serious illness, neither the past nor the future becomes an accessible psychological dimension: memories could be painful, and projects by now impossible. Besides, since often accused to have caused the present illness, the own past is pregnant of tragedies, and could not constitute a moment of relief. Similarly, a focus on the future time, as we have already seen, cannot be suggested. For that reason, a sick person could feel "imprisoned" in the present time when, instead, s/he should find a meaning in it. The same happens in the characters of the book by Camus: "Impatient of their own present, hostile for the own past, and deprived of future, they [*people with plague*; my italics] were similar to those people who are confined behind the bars by the justice".[105]

4.13. THE WITNESSES

Seeing the world always as fresh and new:
this is the aim of a spiritual knowledge.

As it regards the people who assist a sick person, it can finally happens that the elevated number of tragedies and pathological events that torment a patient are, by them, considered as almost *normal and familiar* events, or, apparently, always equal, as if in reality there were no evident and inexorable declines, but only a status of no-comfort. Thus, parents, doctors, nurses, and counselors cannot avoid habits and routines that disguise, instead, a progressive deterioration of the sick person's malaise and health.

Then, a patient becomes aware, as the character of Camus, that: "[...] his/her interlocutor and he do not speak about the same thing. *The sick person* (my italics and note), in fact, expresses himself by the end of long days of rumination and sufferings, and the image that he wants to be communicated warms up for a long time at the fire of the delay and the passion; the other people imagines, instead, a conventional emotion, the pain that is sold in the shops, *a conventional melancholy* (my italics)".[106] Consequently, a process of habituation and adaptation may take out from counseling, freshness and interest, with a detrimental effect on the efficacy of each counselor.

Figure 20 – The cross and delight of spiritual counseling in hospital. The risk of becoming too familiar with a client and his condition might, instead, lower the efficacy of the counseling therapy. In addition, a constant contact with similar pathologies and sufferings, might indeed, implement in counselors a process of familiarity with a disease. This becomes detrimental for the own emotional involvement, adding the risk of becoming skeptical about the outcomes of patients' psychological and spiritual progression. Although being accepting and loving is the spiritual dimension of counseling, at times, under undue stress, the opposite can happen, and a helper assumes provoking attitudes towards the self and the others. This cross or circle is dynamic, and the same counselor might shift from one pole to another depending on his/her own resilience, training, and attitudes.

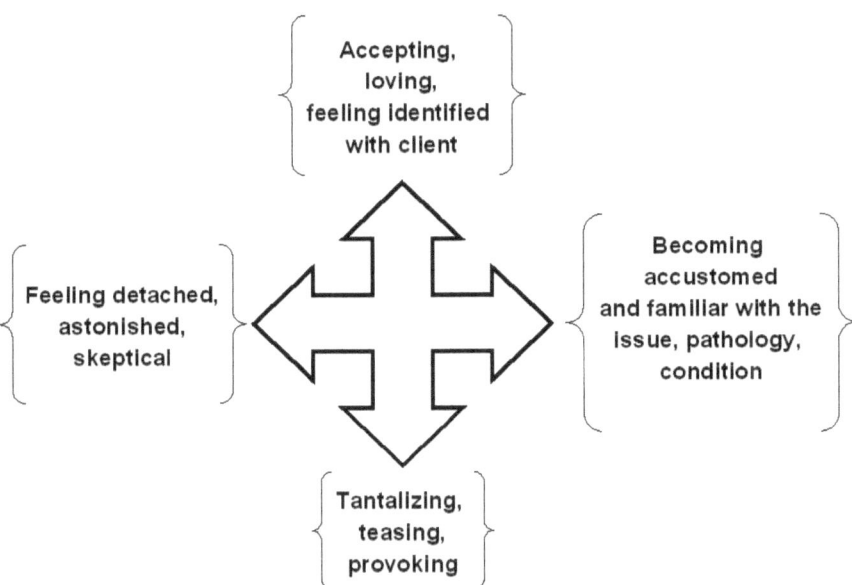

5

The relationship in spiritual counseling

✦

5.1. WORDS TO INFUSE COURAGE

> *The words from your heart*
> *are like a fireplace*
> *in the life of afflicted souls.*

Each spiritual counselor shall be familiar with a vocabulary ready-help to keep in mind and to use as a guide when supporting patients. Someone might have beautiful words, which make glad the people to whom they are said, like: "Good! Well done!", "Came on, I like what you do!". Other words, apparently innocents, instead it is better not saying because they are not a real spiritual and psychic help. Like: "You are the usual lazy man", "You are a weak person!", "Move on!". Even if someone uses them to infuse courage, instead, s/he can accomplish the opposite effect. In fact, these words turn out offensive for people who listen to them. Last, there are words clearly lethal, off-limit, which create a kind of emotional shock to whom listens to them: "When you cry you seem a child to me!". Perhaps this person has just lost a dear person, he has been fired, s/he has been diagnosed a cancer. Some counselors could inadvertently contribute to the pain of who is in crisis, when they try to speak rather than to understand the real nature of a problem, and to act with lightening sentences. As we will also see afterwards, people need to receive, instead, courage and love.

Communication in spiritual counseling is thus based on a respectful communication of love and on consideration of ill persons. In fact, suffering people try to obtain compassion and strength through words of care and love, through participation in community activities, as masses, pilgrimages, and spiritual activities. Nevertheless, when a spiritual counselor form bonds with a client, s/he will appear as a true guide to client's eyes, or more exactly, like a person who not only has technical capacities to help but also human and spiritual gifts for doing so. Then, if we want to develop our social intelligence we will have also to understand how people use religion and prayer to give a sense to their life, and to become more resilient to adversities. Prof. Samuel Z. Klausner of the Columbia University in his article *Social Psychology of Courage*, explains that people universally need courage because of the existential anxiety inherent life, thus, solidarity and prayer in religious institutions provide a central support. In fact, according to Prof. Klausner, through community participation to religious ceremonies, meetings, and prayers a person has a temporary relief from daily problems without necessarily acting on the same ones.[107]

Always according to the Prof. Samuel Z. Klausner, solidarity is symbolized by the physical convergence of people in meetings, pilgrimages, or religious ceremonies. This, associated to rhythms, liturgies, and hymns that unify many voices, reduces the distance between people and communities.[108] Finally, Prof. Klausner thinks that a social unification is accompanied by an internal mobilization of psychic energies and, therefore, by an increase of courage.[109] Therefore, when we go back to the case of a relationship with a tormented person, a central point is the infusion of courage allowing the birth of solidarity and a feeling of support between a counselor and a patient. Similarly, as in religious rituals, also spiritual counseling is infused of the same contents. Here, a helper and the broken-hearted person, through a progressive and reciprocal involvement, arrive to create rules and rituals of mutual support and reciprocal respect. How to say it? It is as if they prayed together!

5.2. How to communicate with a sick person[110]

Not always is spirituality a spontaneous development during life crises. You need to work hard to reach spiritual peaks.

The sudden death of a dear person is always accompanied by a deep suffering. The same affliction is present in a person who has just learned to have a serious illness. Other people have similar reactions by knowing that they have been abandoned from a dear person. Losses are a component of our daily experiences, but, at the same time, when facing serious and terminal illnesses we experience our narrowness, and our impotence in front of events that partially we can overcome. This awareness becomes more painful when we acknowledge a lack of meaning in our life able to transcend what is daily and physical. During these events, we search for an inner purpose that can be everlasting, transcendent, spiritual, and therefore metaphysical.

Thus, again, panic, anxiety, etc., all belong to our humanity anyhow, to our corruptible and, thus, "terminal" nature. Besides, a circumstantial game of hopelessness and serenity, pain and joy, are present, in the existence of who knows that in a short while, life will ask him to surrender what is left: hope, days, affections, safety. In this transaction from the bank of the most complete feeling of safety, suddenly we move to a deep darkness. Meanwhile we all cross benches of fog of indecision that seem temporarily broken by the warm rays of the sun. Suddenly, the eyes of a patient become acquainted with what is dark and gray, an icy scenery that pierces through the bones. Shivers characterize this moment because of the prickly cold and of the loneliness that reside constant in the lands of the no-return and no-hope. By now serenity, warmth, certainty, as also the belief to be able to succeed, all belong to the past. Of this last some memoirs remain, perhaps only some words said by other people who have crossed a man's walk. However, other patients continue their own religious, spiritual, psychological way to life, also whereas darkness reigns. Yet, nobody will feel more the same. Indeed, each one sees with different eyes what once seemed useless and ordinary. To this renewed person, other equals appear under a different light: "I don't understand them anymore. All those things that once seemed so important, now, appear so useless and paradoxical". The world appears with this new perception to whom is overcoming a crisis, or to whom is aware that s/he does not belong anymore to the world of people who still long for the eternity.

Consequently, a seriously ill person does not accept to any condition to identify himself/herself in the values and in the beliefs of the majority that, to him, seem so "ordinary" and so "vague", deprived of any chance to represent the salt of life. Also the apprenticeship of who sees the own death and the end with the own eyes is rapid. Moreover, even the own existential decision is double: reality is either not accepted and the ill person pretends not to see and to feel, or s/he takes on him/her the responsibility to see and to feel. In reality, we can be surprised to discover how many people are able to overcome moments of crisis and discouragement by returning to a serenity that, instead, does not show the deep changes in the own spirit and in the own mind. However, something is changed forever. They are the feelings that feed themselves of a new food that, who has not suffered, would never be able to taste on the Earth. Indeed, an incurable disease, a moral or a physical pain, an abandonment and an isolation, a suffered violence, poverty, the insecurity for tomorrow, a scorn, a serious illness, they are all events that leave so deep traces that a person who has suffered them will look at life in a different way, forever. S/he will be reflexive. S/he will select people and things. S/he will answer with very acute feelings, very deep emotions.

At this point, it becomes evident to affirm that who takes a seat in front of a very ill patient does not have other alternative than abandoning his/her own pre-arranged mental schemes. Thus, a counselor will have to welcome a person whose vision of the world can astonish the counselor itself. This makes the relationship with a terminal patient an irreplaceable moment. In fact, in the dyad counselor-patient, a unique experience develops. Here, there are not schemes, solid theories, and certainties. Practically, everything will have to be invented. All must be created from the beginning. This makes this encounter very difficult for a counselor, and, at the same time, so real and deep, so awful in its immediateness, while a discouragement sometimes torments also the most experienced helper.

Practically, spiritual counseling can represent an opportunity to convey to a person who suffers, through the gestures and the words of a helper, a sign of comfort, of grief, of liking, and of hope. Indeed, all it takes is, sometimes, convincing the client to understand that we are really listening to him/her while s/he is speaking about his/her affliction, to complete the greater part of spiritual counseling. It would be an inappropriate belief for a counselor "to listen, and to be interested in" without painful consequences, neither can s/he assume that the exposure to the contents of a person in mourning can be met without a suitable spiritual, professional, and personal preparation. Often, in the helping relationships of very sick patients, unexpected emotional and communicative peaks are touched. In fact, the bond between counselors and clients is a dynamic alternation of hopes and frustrations, of joy and pain. Furthermore, in the moments of help a helper shall abstain from expressing hasty judgments on the tactics that a client uses for answering to the own tragedy, and to the own unusual emotions.

Even if the causes of a crisis are comprehensible, the subjective reactions of an ill patient betray every theoretical prediction. Indeed, these reactions represent and absorb at any given time all the emotions, and are a fusion of a present distress mixed to life story, and worries about future. Consequently, every expression of pain is comprehensible if we observe its historical frame, read its implication in the present, and decode it with its future value. Anything in life is put again in discussion: patient's values, beliefs, and relationships with other people. Some patient almost reaches a schizoid division between the own past identity, of healthy person, and the present one of sick person. Often s/he hardly recognizes himself/herself in his/her past identity, and has difficulty to take on the present identity. It is a moment of confusion, a limbo of uncertainty about the Self.

In any way, a patient sometimes succeeds in managing the own emotions when s/he had some experience about them. Nevertheless, how can he or she live new and unique emotional experiences? The immanent one, and the incommensurable one often paint all new emotional experiences of a patient. Moreover, despite their neatness, the unpredictability of emotions is destructive: who is victim of these "acute emotional reactions" often is not able to foretell how events will evolve. Usually, the spirit becomes the master of emotions. Hence, it does not care what mind does because ratiocination is overpowered by strong emotions. Constantly, under undue stresses, a patient "knows that s/he is ill, very ill, etc., without "believing it". A constant experience, especially in people seriously ill, is "to hardly believe" that something is really happening. Practically, during a strong emotional turmoil linked to illnesses, believing and knowing are separated: a person "can know something without believing it". This is a common split between emotions and intelligence, hearth and mind, here-and-now and hope found in any subject who has a serious pathology. Therefore, spiritual counseling of ill patients is mainly based on the reality of emotions, more that on the unavoidability of facts. For a counselor this also means accepting and interacting with patients that show high degrees of emotional containment, joy, and resilience, in spite of their poor medical records. At times, also the opposite is true, like the counseling of patients with strong emotional reactions to acceptable medical conditions.

In addition, a feeling with which a spiritual counselor will have to work is the feeling of shame that strikes many patients. People who see illness and death as a defeat of their own spiritual and religious life are more upset. The same happens to those patients who believe to have some responsibilities in the development of their own pathology. The accepting attitude of a counselor is thus central for the help of patients that normally develop some degree of self-critique.

Finally, let us consider that we usually need consolidated techniques to assist silent patients. In effect, it is not easy for a counselor to remain in silence in front of the desperation of a person who does not succeed in expressing himself or in making himself clear. Sometimes, a counselor projects onto patients his/her own anguishes. Thus, the way a counselor has to silence his/her own emotional resonance of client's suffering, is to talk a lot, to cover patient's expressions, and to launch "beauty" expressions in order to "distract" the patient from painful thoughts and phrasing. This is the sign that a spiritual counselor is afraid to be very involved in the idea of death and dying because afraid him/herself. However, at this point, a new insight is needed, together with a clear awareness of the own professional inclinations.

Finally, each stage of elaboration of a loss is characterized by a total psychic collapse. During the initial stages of mourning, we can witness a prevailing introspection and isolation of a patient from the rest of the world. Normally, the periods following the initial shock (notification of a diagnosis, recent surgical operation, beginning of an anti-cancer therapy) are characterized by the return of interests toward the external world. Thus, by suggesting to patients an employment of their time in philanthropic activities we can facilitate this process. Indeed, altruistic actions, that fully re-enters among spiritual and philanthropic strategies, usually help a person to move the focus of his/her own attention from the self toward the world, understood in a general sense: the others, self in relationship with other people, family, affections, but also religion, prayer, and care of the self. In this sense, a patient should be seen as a spiritual/physical being aiming to develop alternative pathways of personal growth for reinforcing the own resilience. As some Authors explain, "Patients present themselves as integrated beings whose physical, emotional and spiritual welfare are entwined".[111]

5.3. BUILDING STRATEGIES FOR SPIRITUAL COUNSELING

> *Sometimes changing focus from*
> *Self to other is spiritual and therapeutic.*
> *Help yourself by helping your neighbors*
> *is the true way to spirituality.*

Counseling in spirituality is always a way in which counselors and clients try to reach higher degrees of adjustment in spite of painful life experiences. This process encompasses the ability of a client to make a partial or total reality test, which, when considering serious pathologies, can be altered because of strong emotional reactions and the refusal to accept what seems unavoidable. Therefore, a counselor can witness several opposite reactions that are always a sign of a deep psychological distress (Tab. 6).

Moreover, philanthropy and altruism are two dimensions of spirituality but also strategies for growth and consolidation of the self. This is even more significant in serious illness since, during the acute stage of crises and losses, patients are concentrated on their own pain and deeds. Practically the self is completely inward focused. On the whole, during these moments, it becomes important to help patients to move their focus outward, usually towards the relationships with other people for reinforcing mutual bonds, and processes of brotherhood and sisterhood. Nevertheless, also in hospital, patients feel a strong need to receive a continuous emotional assistance from other people in the community, or even to offer it when health conditions would allow it. It is the case of hospitalized mothers who like to have around the whole family to emotionally assist their children.

As a result, in hospital or at home, patients who can feel helpful for others and their plights can find some extra energy and overcome their own crises. Thus, an *altruistic and philanthropic dimension, which fully responds to a stage of spiritual growth, is also a way to find a recovery from desperation and losses. It is up to a spiritual counselor to promote this plan as a true therapeutic instrument for many people who are suffering, and that are still very focused on their own tragedy and disease. In addition, an activation of a philanthropic-altruistic inclination in patients, is fully respectful of a their dignity, and does not raise defense mechanisms and unexpected emotional reactions. Basically, this corresponds to a strategy of "Help others for helping yourself".*

According to Cervantes & Parham, we shall consider the healing power of community interconnectedness and interpersonal help that should be addressed by community counselor. In fact, according to these Authors, "There is an increased trust and belief in brotherhood and sisterhood in which there is co-participation and responsibility to community healing".[112]

Besides, as the Table 8 will show, there are certain personal and community skills that a spiritual person uses in order to take care of the self and others.

Table 6 – Emotions caused by a loss, and a spiritual way to cope with a disease.

A way...	... and its opposite	A spiritual way
Anger against oneself.	Anger against other people.	Not blaming anyone.
Depression.	Apparent indifference.	Using emotions for personal growth and fortification.
Fear and block of decisions.	Assuming an overactive role (doing for not thinking).	Being active in doing things important for self and others.
Weeping and desperation.	Apparent coldness.	Warmth and depth in emotional reactions.
Wish to be helped continuously at no conditions.	Apparent refusal of assistance.	Intention to be helpful: to be helped but, at the same time, to help.
Search of what has been lost.	Resignation to the loss.	Search of alternative and spiritual resources to replace the principal loss.
Search of a distraction.	Impossibility to be detached from present events, and to take a breath.	A use of reality to coordinate efforts for an ongoing growth.
Looking always to photos.	Elimination of all the memoirs.	Clients use autobiography for the self-discovery of historical-existential meanings and their "place in the world".
Search for grief.	Refusal of grief and jealousy of one's own feelings: the attitudes of other people lived by clients as a façade of etiquette.	Acceptance of grief and closeness by others as a sign of connectedness.

Table 7 – Certainties and doubts in hospitalized patients, in parents, and in relatives

A way...	... and its opposite	A spiritual counseling
Certainty, from the family, about the causes of illness and death of a sick parent and relative.	Suspect from the family about the causes of illness and death of a sick parent and relative.	A counselor helps family, friends, and relatives to adjust to death, and assists them in having a satisfying version of the truth. In case of malpractice, s/he helps parents and relatives to feel understood and protected.
A patient has the certainty that physicians, health personnel, and hospital have done all their possible.	A patient suspects that physicians and hospital have neglected important parts in diagnosis and therapy.	A counselor works for a therapeutic alliance and to participate to the version proposed by patients and relatives. Although not functioning as "judge", a spiritual counselor meets client's emotional expressions to make him/her feel protected and supported.
A patient blames him/herself for the causes and the progression of the own illness.	A patient apparently blames none.	A patient becomes respectful of self and others.
A patient accepts diagnosis and treatment.	A patient refuses diagnosis and treatment.	A counselor helps clients to reduce inward fury to operate with a different truth plan: reconstructing life and priorities.
A patients seeks help from others, parents, and relatives.	A patient prefers silence and conceals the own condition.	A client becomes open to share and to accept interpersonal relationships without hiding. S/he lives the assistance from other people as a true sign of love and respect without developing feelings of shyness.

Table 8 – Spiritual skills for self and others, and for clients and counselors.

Skills based on being	Skills based on doing to self	Skills based on doing to others
Respectful	Respectful to the self	Respectful to others
Loving	Taking care of the self	Taking care of others
Undemanding	Being simple towards the self	Being simple towards others
Differentiated but not individualist	Accepting the self as it is, with the aim to get better	Accepting others as they are, with the aim to grow together, towards higher degrees of spiritual well-being and shared support
Philanthropic	Reducing hedonism	Investing time and efforts to raise the well-being of underprivileged people in a spirit of brotherhood and sisterhood
Leadership	Using power to increase insight in self and others	Using leadership to promote social advancement and mutual understanding
Accepting	Accepting mistakes as a way to progress	Accepting others' mistakes as a way to understanding and to closeness to groups
Guidance	Accepting any guidance as a way to self-disclosure	Accepting to be a guide if this is done for a mutual growth
Prayer	A way of self discovery and healing	A way to reinforce community bonds and shared healing

Next, we will find important strategies to use with clients in order to offer them the best assistance when presenting with serious illnesses and crises. Practically, in hospital there are many people and circumstances that a counselor meets:

- A client before the diagnosis of a serious/terminal illness.
- A client after the diagnosis of a serious/terminal illness.
- Parents and relatives of a patient.
- Hospitalized patients.
- Potential clients in a waiting list.
- Any person directly or indirectly involved with a client: e.g., family doctor, personal pastor, friends, philanthropic institutions, etc.

Usually, the moments that immediately precede and follow a diagnosis of a serious illness, determine a shock in a person and an extreme vulnerability and sensitiveness to every kind of intervention and communication addressed to this client, even if used with the best intentions. Thus, spiritual counseling is an opportunity to deliver to a patient, through gestures and words, signs of comfort, of grief, of liking of which this person feels a lot the need. In these moments, a counselor also has to abstain from hasty judgments on the emotional reactions used by patients to answer to their own tragedy. In fact, a counselor would not be able to find any equivalence between what he considers to be "normal" reactions to pain, and the personal manner of patients to answer to what is happening to them. Besides strategies of listening, counselors might need further training in facing clients' silence. Some, in fact, have the tendency to privilege a dimension less involved, eliminating the moments of silence during any relationship, thus, tending to talk instead of listening to distressed patients. Indeed, it is normal to feel uneasy in front of patients that remain mute. As a result, some counselors runs over these patients with a plethora of information and words, so to avoid more delicate and painful matters, but also because they have difficulty in managing the language of feelings. Therefore, as Prof. Harold Koenig affirms: "Listening with respect and concern may be all that is needed".[113]

5.4. THE GRADIENT OF THE NEWS

In spirituality
there is more soul
than brain.

We need to consider that the ambassadors of sad news are not often seen favorably by anybody. Pain and tragedy, even if served on a silver dish, are always difficult to be elaborated. This also because bad news often arrive unexpected. From here, the perplexity of many counselors: "And now how can I tell to this patient that s/he has a serious illness?". At this point, I think that a good strategy is to give sad news with gradualness, respecting the times of a patient and offering only the truth without eliminating elements of hope. Besides, news that are given for first have to be those that offer more hope: for instance the existence of a certain therapy, the commitment of the medical personnel to do its best, the existence of other hospitals for a better care, etc. Only when a client has gotten used to this new reality it is possible to deliver other information without overloading of data patients and their families. Besides, also the elements of hope must be given with ratiocination to avoid that behind the pressures of a patient, counselors or doctors give encouraging but false information to the only purpose to avoid an emotional breakdown already in action.

Nevertheless, the habit to give "very" encouraging information can also hide an unconscious difficulty of counselors and medical personnel to manage their own anguish about death and dying. Indeed, this way, they favors the thirst of hope of a sick person, and avoid saying: "Your situation needs care and attention", or "It is important that you really know that...", etc. Furthermore, the doors for insight in distressed patients are very narrow, thus, only few and important information can pass those doors at any given time. In addition, *no matter how intense is the participation of counselors in the process of explaining sad news, any patient will usually chose independently how much to understand, to believe, to hope, and to lose heart.* It is for these reasons, and because it is instinctive and human in these conditions to filter only those news that patients feel able to manage, that the spiritual counseling and the helping relationship to the terminal patient is always a process of waiting, listening, and temporizing. This breaks with the traditional counseling process where the aim is to focus on reality testing and understanding. On the contrary, *spiritual counseling of terminal patients is based on a different level of reality: spiritual reality. Practically a new interpretation and ontology of reality, which is foreign to any familiar concept we might have about reality as a whole.* We shall then leave free any patient to use any psychological defense mechanisms s/he feels important to use in order to reduce, or limit, a mounting desperation and worry. Moreover, it is all right for counselors even accepting a superficial madness of clients who are striving to readjust their internal world on a different wavelength. In the following paragraphs we shall examine the strategies for the management of silence when dealing with distressed persons.

5.5.   THE MANAGEMENT OF SILENCE

Silently speaking to the soul.
This is the true force for
interpersonal bonds.

Being in front of a desperate person, facing the silence and the weeping of it, is not an easy job for counselors. Rather, some have the tendency to fill the moments of silence by trying comments and phrases for helping. Nevertheless, patient's silence is a very deep and incisive message of a moment of anguish and desperation, thus it should be accepted and honored as an important expression of his/her feelings. However, silence itself might generate counter-transference feelings in counselors. Furthermore, depending on the personal scripts and experiences of counselors themselves, they can feel nervous when dealing with a patient who does not offer spontaneous accounts about the own thoughts, worries, and feelings. That is why many counselors show a tendency to speak as soon as a few seconds of silence are passed. Some break the silence by furnishing other information. Others try to say something but are confused about what is better to do.

At the beginning, a good footstep for counselors it is to discover what meaning has the silence for them. A practical approach to spiritual counseling is also the management of patient's silence. Moreover, it is central to understand what meanings have for a patient, the silence and the non-verbal communication in the self and others. During stressful events, any patient is able to filter, from inner and outer reality, only few things, information, words, and gestures. Consequently, counselors shall not expect from clients a full development and elaboration of internal turmoil and worries. This generates a sort of apparent paucity in external manifestations of patient's feelings. The end result is that words about feelings and emotions (generally an important part in normal counseling setting), in hospital might have a different quality, quantity or even lack completely. Thus, silence, and the interpretation of silence (that can become "words of spirit") acquire a different meaning and management during spiritual counseling.

In these moments, only few hints would be externally evident. Even the whole spiritual and internal dialogue of a patient may be so personal to be concealed also during sections of spiritual counseling. Consequently, any action of support is basically implanted on "soft" gestures and words, on "spiritual mottos", on "short religious citations", which have more possibilities to be accepted by a mourning person. The relationship of help to the seriously ill patient and to the anguished person is rather characterized by moments in which words seldom constitute the central part of the interaction. Indeed, spiritual counseling is rather a passage of "something beautiful between two persons" perhaps by osmosis, with a gradient that goes from the person who is more spiritual (counselor or patient) to the person who is less spiritual (counselor or patient). From here, we can easily understand why spirituality and religion are not a talk of mouth but a talk of hearths. For example, all the centers for cult and spiritual inspiration are, indeed, places of silence and meditation. Consequently also spiritual counseling is a moment of peace and reflection.

Patient's situational silence must therefore be respected and used during counseling as moment of dialogue among hearts, and of strengthening of affective assonances. During the moments of silence and meditation, the bonds between counselors and patients are strengthened. Besides, also through the respect of the silence and the grief in patients, a counselor allows them to spiritually grow and to mature stronger defenses. Consequently, a respectful position of counselors, avoids a dominant position not applicable in spiritual counseling. Moreover, in spiritual counseling, what assume particular relief are the phonetic aspects of the words, the tone of the voice that accompanies the gestures of proximity and care but also the management of silence.

Practically, gestures of caring, that we already know, in spiritual counseling must be improved. It is not enough to simply offer a glass of water, a pleasant place, and a tissue paper. Indeed, non-verbal communication totally responds to the ethical and practical requirements of spiritual counseling. Essentially, a mix of silence, words, gestures all addressed to convey the idea of caring, respect, and love. This way what counts more is what counselors "do" with patients. Practically, the rhythm of the melody that slowly develops during the interaction, and signed by the triad *words-gestures-silence* (WGS) increases the credibility of counselors to the eyes of their clients. Indeed, spiritual counselors, like water on flowers, promote the development of clients' inner forces and progression to spontaneous (spiritual) healing. This "spontaneous growth of patient's spirituality" was also a concern for Viktor Frankl who commented: "The authentic religiousness, if existential, must have time to emerge spontaneously. A man could never be pushed to it".[114]

Larry Culliford indicates the spirituals skills in a person, which, I believe, can apply either to counselors or patients:[115]

- Being able to create a state of mind based on peace and tranquility.

- Being able to be focused on the present, and the here and now.

- Developing an attitude to empathy, sensitivity, and fearlessness.

- Developing an attitude to survive during distress while developing a parallel attitude of hope.

- Developing an attitude to be honest with self especially when irritated, worried or hesitant.

- Being able to develop generosity without feeling exhausted.

- Being able to grieve appropriately and let go.

5.6. SPIRITUAL COUNSELING IS NOT AN INVESTIGATION

*Spiritual quest is not
an inspection.
It is a warm acceptance
of any diversity.*

In spiritual counseling and in helping relationships, enquiries serve only for promoting self-exploration in a client. In the following stages, this is useful to strengthen the strategies of self-healing and self-caring. However, subsequently, enquires from a counselor during encounters with clients, decrease or totally disappear. Especially in the stage of desperation, it is not suitable to use questions while a patient is following his/her own anguish. Neither a counselor has to use investigations because s/he has only to acquire professional data. What has to prevail is, instead, an explanatory, indirect, empathic, and synergic approach:

*   *Explanatory*, because a counselor tries to put a "word" to what a client is expressing. If a patient says: "I feel a terrible stomach ache when I think about it", the counselor can try: "So, it is like you're telling me about your sense of emptiness. Is it so?".

*   *Indirect*, because there is an effort by a counselor to use indirect expressions and questions: "I wonder if you like to share with me what you're feeling in this moment", instead of "How do you feel?".

*   *Empathic*, here refers to the fact that a counselor might, at times, try some verbal expression reflecting how a silent client is feeling in that moment. For example, with a calm voice in front of a distressed patient: "It is not easy in moment likes this to talk because of the pain in one's soul". Usually, a client will eventually complete counselor's interpretations that do not totally explain his/her silence: "A part the pain it is also the feeling of loneliness". One small phrase I have used with success can be: "It is not easy to face these moments. You feel as if God and others abandoned you. Alternatively, that the world is falling on you. However, perhaps there are some possibilities to feel better, to find something that can give you back a sense to your life even if now it does not seem to have it. Please consider that I am

available to walk together to you in this path, because it is easier if it is done together".

- *Synergic*, because a counselor respects client's energy, time, pace, and pauses. By no means will a counselor go beyond client's rhythm of self-disclosure. For example, a counselor who displays an extra-energy during patient's explanation of deep weakness. Alternatively, a counselor is talkative when a client can hardly send out few words.

The attitude to investigate and to gather data, instead of focusing on the relationship, can also hide an underlying difficulty in counselors to accept an interview or interaction with patients of whom they apparently know a little, especially "how clients could emotionally react". Truly, we all are acquainted with the psychological reactions during a loss, a diagnosis of a severe disease, and hospitalization. Nevertheless, counselor's "fear to face an unknown person" can hide a basic obstacle to accept closeness and sharing as a complementary pathway to healing and caring. That is why some inexpert counselors, stay ossified on querying positions asking to their distressed clients all the hows, whys, whens, etc. Usually, in helping relationships and in spiritual counseling health practitioners are more flexible and elastic in accepting clients because their starting viewpoint is that "The other fellow is a distressed brother or sister", or more, "There are not many alternatives to aid an aching and suffering human being but to rescue him or her from pain and loneliness". That is why spiritual help in the health system or community is an absolute approach to the "unknown" suffering brother and sister, by this meaning an absence of verbal and non-verbal enquiries (of the kind: "What's your name? How old are you? Where do you come from? Why are you here? Etc.). In a word, *during spiritual counseling, the existence of another human being is enough for beginning a mutual understanding and helping, although there are few or no "demographical" data about the other needy fellow.*

5.7. THE MANAGEMENT OF EMOTIONS IN COUNSELORS

*Spirituality means
perceiving the self-with-others
during a mutual
movement of growth
and healing.*

Often, a counselor wonders if it is correct to feel emotions of stress, suffering, sorrow, or even refusal towards a suffering person. The fear of a counselor is that these reactions to patients and their illnesses might create a separation more than an approach. Furthermore, a counselor might believe that as specialist it is not correct to be overwhelmed by emotions of separation, or that it is always appropriate to conceal one's own reactions to the illness of the own patient. In short, that is correct also to hide negative reactions as counselor's own anger, desperation in consequence of the frustration during the progression of an illness, or during the decline of health in the own patient. Some counselors believe that it is important to show always a smile, and the maximum inclination to accept anything from a patient, or to reveal always the better side of the self. The risk, however, is that the relationship might become twisted, deprived of spontaneity, and, to the eyes of a patient, emptied of sincerity. Instead, spiritual counseling is a relationship "among people" that are excited, worried, happy in unison. Basically, counselors and patients, walk together during an encounter of sincere sharing of emotions, affections, and support. In order to create a fluid relationship, a counselor has to establish strategies not to cover the own feelings but, rather, to use them as a resource for the care of a patient. This can implicate, sometimes, that a counselor expresses his/her own feelings of the here-and-now to a patient, "I am sorry that this is happening to you", or, "By listening at your words I feel in myself a kind of uneasiness, I wonder if this is something that you already know". These expressions about the "what" and "how" a counselor perceives the relationship are very useful tools to help a patient to make contact with his/her own feelings. In addition, counselor's self-disclosure helps patients to increase their own insight about personal and interpersonal emotions produced by their state of health and pain.

Spiritual counseling is thus an equilibrated and respectful interaction between two people holding, each one, an equal importance during an interpersonal encounter. Although in standard counseling, a counselor might behave from a standpoint of higher differentiation, sometimes promoting the existence of a setting with a neat separation in the parts counselor/client, this partition, in spiritual counseling, does not represent a therapeutic requirement because sharing is much more important than distinction.

5.8. THE PATIENT'S BOND WITH THE LOST OBJECT

Be kind and full of consideration
for your patient
and half therapy will be done.

During a deep psychological suffering, a person would be able not to see any way out from what is happening. If a patient has just known to have a serious illness, then s/he will not accept anything of what happens, and consequently, s/he might also refuse to approve any psychological help, because this means recognizing to have something worrisome. Then, a resistance to accept counseling can be framed as a defense mechanism, mainly when a person is picking up his/her own energies not to suffer more. A counselor should thus accept these moments, and should not force a patient to accept an offer of sessions of counseling. Moreover, a helper needs a lot of patience, especially if a patient is still in the stage of incredulity and anger for what is happening. In this stage, it is not suitable to offer further information to clients. Instead, what will count more will be a natural predisposition of a counselor to non-verbal relationships and communications. Which means that a helper will have to manage long moments of silence, of anger, of void in patients, by speaking the less possible but by showing gestures of protection, of gentleness, and of welcoming. A lot also depends on patient's familiarity with spirituality and religion. In fact, some Authors found that spiritual counseling could be the central therapy of depressed patients, especially if they are very religious Christians.[116]

Table 9 – Verbal and non-verbal skills in spiritual counseling. Whatever is the choice, counselors will act as facilitators, and promoters of patient's inner growth and self-discovery.

Non verbal skills in spiritual counseling	Verbal skills in spiritual counseling
Listening.	Talking less than a client.
Being gentle.	Using only encouraging words.
Staying aside a client while suffering.	Whispering words while staying close clients.
Protecting clients if unable to take care of themselves.	Being resolute and not showing hesitancy in the words.
Doing something valuable but simple for clients: e.g. offering a hand, helping to walk, and assisting to feed.	Self-disclosure if indicated.
"Talking" softly to patient even if apparently unheard.	Saying pleasant words related to patient's relatives and friends.

Apart from emotionally sustaining a patient, a counselor will also have to furnish to patients some information on what is happening. Therefore, although a helper is exempt from providing reserved medical information, s/he can still receive some vital queries by patients who are trying to understand some central deeds in their life as, for instance, "Am I dying"?, "How much remains me to live"?, etc. In addition, a physician and a nurse can be counselors, and in this case, they are designed to supply more information. When one speaks to patients about difficult matters, it is a good norm to always use some metaphors, better if taken by a context familiar to patients. Then it is important to resort to words and comprehensible explanations and to avoid a technical jargon. It is important also to remember that during an acute crisis, a patient does not have the whole attention focused on what is told to him/her. For such reason it is necessary to attend that he is calmer, and, however the counselor must not flood him or her of words and information. When a counselor desires to deliver data that help a patient to make him/her feel better, s/he will have to illustrate the same concepts more times in a row. Which means that a counselor must not get tired to repeat the same information so many times respecting both the pace of understanding of a patient and his/her desire of "not wanting to know more".

5.9. A COUNSELOR SHOULD KNOW HIMSELF

Scrutinize your heart,
decipher your mind,
control your soul,
clear your eyes.
All this is spiritual.

A basic rule for counseling seriously ill patients is that a counselor shall know his/her own reactions to losses and mourning. Only when starting from this awareness a helper will succeed in tuning with patients who face serious, chronic, and terminal illnesses. Another painful experience for a spiritual counselor is that of not being totally accepted by clients.

In a research, it emerged that Christian patients seldom accept a relationship with secular counselors, these patients being afraid that these counselors are less sensitive than Christian or spiritual counselors. In addition these patients are afraid to be misinterpreted by counselors who have not a specific spiritual and religious training.[117] Moreover, patients in general might be concerned that Christian counselors can try to influence their ideas and values.[118]

However, if a counselor is sincere with him/herself and with his/her client, then s/he can also overcome some common places or stereotyped behaviors dictated more by one role of his/her than by the demands of counseling. How to say? "Being more human and less professional towards clients". In fact many counselors believe that a rigid rule exists in the "professional behavior". They might also assume that there is an obligation to appear "cold and detached" in front of death and patients' sufferings. Nevertheless, this brings counselors to hide and to suffocate their own emotions, and not to a healthy opening toward the movement of their own soul: basically the core of their own spirituality. Indeed, some Authors have shown that is the counselor's openness the trigger for a client to discuss religious and spiritual matters.[119]

Sometimes, physiological as well as biochemical changes in the body homeostasis are also implied in enhancing negative reactions of patients to their own surroundings. This way some strong emotions in bereaved patients are depression associated to anger, a strong feeling of guilt, social isolation, desire to remain alone, envy toward healthy people, and fear to remain without the basic health assistance because of personal, financial, or family causes. When a spiritual counselor meets these people s/he has also to accept patient's resistances to talk or to be assisted as a way that a client has to restore a sense of mastery and power in life, when everything seems showing an inexorable decline of the own life. For this reason, a spiritual counselor, more than any other health specialist, makes of the acceptance of the other fellows his/her own central point of strength.

5.10. THE STAGES OF SPIRITUAL GROWTH

> *Spiritual growth*
> *is like the blossoming*
> *of flowers.*
> *So gradual! So smooth!*

The choice of the philosopher Seneca is not casual. In fact, he is amongst the few authors that face the theme of life by treating the issue of death and dying. This is central when it is necessary to talk about a person who shows to be skeptical in believing that during a short life there are still some chances to be serene. Thorough the words of Seneca we can derive also the stages of spiritual growth that can be subdivided in:

- *Pre-spiritual stage.–* A client has not started a spiritual quest yet. The existences of an acceptable state of health, or even continuous medical check-ups, have not raised any need for a spiritual assistance yet.

- *Stage of spiritual awareness.–* A client feels that "something" is missing in his/her life, but s/he is unable to transform this feeling into a spiritual pathway. Nevertheless, a patient, that is not recent to a diagnosis of illness, starts to appreciate "simplicity and daily" things, people, and activities, as enabling to achieve a certain degree of joy. This person searches the fullness of life through daily living. This can also be identified as a stage of spiritual mentality that can be improved in further stages.

- *Stage of discouragement and emptiness.–* A patient might have moments of apprehension during an intractable pain or complex therapy. Chronic fatigue and malaise can weaken the constancy for spiritual growth. However, the perception of a limited life or existential expectancy can function as a force for spiritual improvement prompted by the search for an "alternative reality to the actual misery".

- *Stage of active spiritual participation.–* A patient starts to appreciate others and community as a valuable force in helping him/her to overcome periods of desperation and loneliness. By an active sharing during relationships, s/he feels that also the own pain can be distributed to other people by "communicating the own feelings, and by reinforcing spiritual bonds". Religious practices, prayers, and other spiritual/religious rituals can help in restructuring life and time. A religious community also helps a patient in talking about death and dying as being part of the awareness that all believers share into that community.

- *Stage of acceptance and enjoyment.*– A patient has accepted his/her own disease, and there is reconciliation with the self and the own body. S/he has time to spend in spiritual matters by participating to groups of prayers, philanthropic events, religious ceremonies, etc. A patient feels that s/he can bring some important contribution of his/hers into community, and uses the actual health condition as a resource for empathizing with people who suffer. Moreover, according to one's own personal creed, sufferings and sorrows are felt as proof of devotion and faith.

In the **pre-spiritual stage** a sick person is still linked to the prevailing culture that imply that, in order to avoid pain and suffering, one should not be bothered with "painful ideas about death and dying". The only alternative during melancholy, in the pre-spiritual stage, seems being a forgetfulness based on *avoiding occupying the own mind with sad thoughts*. The goal for a counselor, helping a patient in the pre-spiritual stage is, to convince him/her that the remaining life still has some chance to be serene. The journey that brings to the discovery of a sense of life, even if it deals with a brief life, is not easy. For the sick person it is strewn of traps, and it is also easy to be discouraged and to give up. In this case, a patient remains in a state of total indifference solely attending that death comes.

Hence, in order to favor an existential and spiritual growth, it is interesting to read the works of Seneca to find some interesting reflections about life and death in general. This Author uses a sincere style, not defended, and stimulates a direct appraisal of important existential themes. One of the more remarkable works of Seneca (4 b. C.) is the book *The Brevity Of the Life (De Brevitate Vitae)* that emphasizes, according to the Author, the fact that human beings make a bad use of the time of their own existence. A suggestion for the pre-spiritual man is of take back his own time to reflect about the self. According to Seneca a man has to give to himself a series of moments to spend on reflecting about his/her own life.[120] What is this time for? The answer is: *to look inside ourselves, to listen to ourselves, in other words, to understand our spiritual and existential depth.* Only this way the pre-spiritual man progresses towards the second stage: *the stage of the awareness of the brevity of life*, or simply, **the stage of awareness.** This is not yet a full research of spiritual avenues, but the existential prompt that can launch the spiritual quest of any person. In this stage, a man realizes that he cannot live as if life did not have to ever end, even if he is not sick. The person who starts to work in the stage of spiritual awareness, wonders how much rooted was in him the idea that his life would have never ended. Practically, during the stage of awareness a sick person abandons an almighty dream as s/he discovers that his/her own life can also end in an unexpected way, before his/her own existential programs. Seneca expressed himself in this way: "It is that you live as if life never had to end, you forget your precariousness, you don't consider the time that has already passed, and you waste it as if you drew it from an inexhaustible reserve".[121]

Afterward, Seneca mentions to the habit of many to procrastinate the moment for a serene life, subjugated from contingent plans, from social competition, from an unsatisfactory job, and from a whole series of daily appointments. All these often estrange a person from a contact with himself, making him to waste that precious time that is necessary, instead, to reserve for a serene reflection about his/her own existence. Seneca comments: "How it is foolish to forget that we are deadly procrastinating to the fifty or sixty years the wise intentions, and to want to start our life to an age that only few succeed in reaching!".[122] Therefore, it is always actual the knot of procrastination! Moreover, it is for a practical reason that a terminal patient, or however, the man in the pre-spiritual stage must be helped to operate choices of projects of almost immediate execution. Much more important, the pre-spiritual person does not have to postpone to the future (for example, a trip to foreign countries), the actions (for example, meeting with an important person), and the intentions (for example, to complete an action for the mankind) from which s/he thinks that his/her own calm and joy can derive.

With the overcoming of the stage of procrastination, we reach the **stage of spiritual appreciation** or, rather, of the actions in the here-and-now that play such an important part in the creation of a personal well-being. During this stage, a patient starts to appreciate everyday life, objects, and people, and to make these things a force for his/her own joy. We are not still in a full spiritual integrated stage, but, through this renovated enjoyment of everyday living, a patient enters in a frame of mind that will help him/her in the appreciation of self and others.

Seneca does not use the term "serenity" but "quiet" or, better, it refers to "quiet life." Translated this into modern terms, he certainly desired to propose a loosening of the usual stress or, however, a renouncement of those daily occasions that often bring discouragement, and from which a man does not succeed to reach a spiritual fullness of life. The joy is not residing in the hope about a best life or, rather, in the good intention to reach only "tomorrow" a state of quiet. Any conscious or unconscious delay, in fact, shows to be a little reliable substitute in giving us a favorable direction to our existence. The example that Seneca offers to us is that of August emperor who was living "[…] in the illusion that the day would have come in which he would have lived only for himself […] [and such thought: *my note*] assuaged his works".[123] A severe comment is addressed by Seneca to Cicero, certainly a wise man, but who defined himself "half-free" confessing the fact to be enslaved by life. Cicero, in fact, "Added to regret the preceding life, complained about the present one, and despaired himself of the future one".[124]

5.11. WHY SHALL WE INCREASE PATIENT'S INSIGHT?

Spiritual men seek
undiscovered routes to the Self
as a way to bring light
into the cave of the fate.

According to Seneca, a man shall become master of his own destiny, however "above the fate"[125] or, at least, free to operate some existential and spiritual choices, and capable to put aside what is his role inside the facts of life that involve him personally. This detail appears interesting, particularly for the terminal patient that often debates himself among two polarities. From one side, for a sort of regressive mechanism, s/he desires "to return child". This favors an aspiration to feeling less responsible for the Self, by assuaging the weight of the awareness about the gravity of the situation. On the other side, there is the task for the counselor to increase "patient's awareness" and insight with the intent to remove him or her from a state of partial separation from, or refusal of the own reality. The aim is to make again the patient master of the own "life", by increasing in him/her the courage and the strength to proceed.

But what are the advantages? We wonder if, instead, it would be better for a client to live in a state of "lesser awareness", in a sort of half-sleepiness, unsophisticated, not surmounted by the quest for higher or more complex psychological and spiritual matters in order to lower also the anguish for death and dying, and to leave to other caretakers the task to be "worried about". Sometimes, also the health personnel, and the psychologists could be tempted to strengthen this state of "forgetfulness and low awareness" in patients with the hope that, consequently, also their "inner" problems become less burdensome. But to a deeper analysis, this attitude to "mitigate patients' phantoms" shown by some health workers could, instead, betray their own struggle to cope with the core themes of death and dying, partially reduced by "projecting on patients" their own anguishes and fears.

The shared bias in the helpers is that a man-patient cannon progress any longer in the own personal psychological and spiritual growth, as if also emotional life were halted by the presence of an existential deadline. Nevertheless, by accepting this theory, both caretakers and patients adhere to the assumption that life is enjoyable as long as it has no time limitation. Moreover, the existence of a disease, or even existential limitations generated by poverty and many loses, would breed the concept that even spirituality is acceptable only when no other incumbencies bother mind and spirit. These whole concepts, however, belong to mechanisms of negation, and not sublimation that is a mature concept in health practice and spiritual counseling. It is thus important for a spiritual counselor to surmount his/her own existential doubts, denial, and fears in order to embrace totally the idea that death and dying are "normal" events in the existence of any human being, also of the caretaker itself.

5.12. LIVING WITH TIME PRESSURE

Spirituality has its own
pace and time.
It usually carries
the rhythms of
of our existential struggles.

By going back to Seneca, we see how the Author underlines what makes the core concern in terminal patients. It is that "time" that constantly bothers thoughts and hopes of any human being facing life and existential limitations. This to the point that the shared bias is: "*absence of disease = time = life*" and "*illness = reduced time = dying*". It would be a problematic strategy to counsel with these two equations in mind. It would be as if a helper counseled a human being as a dead person and not as a man or woman that can still totally embrace life, plenitude, and joy. However, also the opposite can be problematic. It is the case of courageous helpers that adopt the strategy of the florist that transforms any suffering and problem into the opposite. Either the "burier" or the "florist" are delicate strategies to maintain, and shall be soon revised for a more mature counseling. For what concerns the importance of time in spiritual counseling we find different uses of time by part of patients:

Table 10 – Time in spiritual counseling. Usually, patient's worries and concerns are somehow joined to time pressure and other issues linked to time.

Way of feeling time	*Ways to treat the time in spirituality*
The time to be	1. To be another or "better" person: e.g., more affective towards family and friends. 2. The time to have a break: from fever, malaise, depression, etc. 3. The time to be good towards the self and the neighbor as related to the own creeds and religion. 4. The time to bring to completion Self-growth and unity.
The time to have	5. To have another chance in life to accomplish some core interest or to perform humanitarian acts. 6. The time to have the opportunity to choose "better" hospitals, doctors, or to try a different/alternative therapy. Particularly linked to the wish to have a better human relationship with staff members.
The time to do	7. The time to do things for other people, to perform acts of remarkable humanitarian meaning if feeling this fact unaccomplished. 8. The time to do something important for the self and the family. 9. The time to arrange things and personal business not to leave the family unattended.
The time to leave	10. The time to leave the own life as a "good person". Thus, the time to leave meaningful traces about the self. 11. The time to make a good impression to community and family. 12. The time to say goodbye to all family and friends.
The time to become	13. The time to become the person s/he always wanted to be. 14. The time to remain "human" when the disease progresses. 15. The time to complete the spiritual preparation and to repair possible moral "lacunas".

For Seneca time is intended as "time for...". Therefore, in the existence of whom identifies with the Self-as-doer, or of whom says "I am, I exist, as long as I succeed in realizing this or that", time becomes a tool of his to act. In other words, a businessman, an artisan or a simple housewife that live for accomplishing their own vital projects based on the "doing", feel spiritually serene and existentially alive as long as they are able "to do" something for the self, for the others, and for the community. It will be therefore an assignment for a counselor to furnish them with the tools to practically accomplish projects based on "doing".

5.13. THE LESSON OF LIFE

> *There is a lot of noise in*
> *our existential turmoil.*
> *There is a peaceful silence*
> *in our spiritual quest.*

Seneca affirms the importance of learning to live, that he makes synonymous to learning to die: "For the whole life we learn to live, as for the whole life we learn to die".[126] In some people there is even the desire to draw near the own death, because they think that only this way it is possible to exorcize the fear that the same arouses. Seneca affirms: "[...] they desire their own death because they fear it".[127] Instead, other people would never like to set term to their moments of thoughtlessness and happiness during which, however, they also set an alarming question: "Up to when it will last?".[128] This last question comprehends the aspiration without measure, the will without thinking that the objects of the own desire can become exhausted or disappear, or that the seduction practiced by them can be darkened by those clouds that already announce, from far away, that to every desire there is a limit set by nothingness or by the impossibility to desire anymore. Consequently, Seneca in his book "*The wise man's constancy*" affirms that: "Invulnerability doesn't consist of not staying stricken, but of not staying wounded".[129]

We could say that this affirmation determines the characteristics of the psychological strategies that some sick people adopt for coming out of their crisis or, rather, "from the being wounded" or from their "wounds". Seneca also speaks about "wound" and not so much of immortality, of absence of pain, or absence of death that, as he affirms, are major conditions of the biological life. However, subsequently, Seneca completes the division between spirit and body. The first one is what has to be valued and fed, and therefore valorized. The body is more short-lived instead, and subject to the laws of time, pain, and corruption. Instead, the "spirit" is in us, in our identity and subjectivity, in our psychology, but it also represents the casket that picks up our sufferings. On the other side, our "body" is subject to death and pain and it is the amphora that produces suffering and worries in the sick person. Any illness, therefore, for its same nature, torments man as body considered as the center for pain receptors generating psychic distress. Seneca, aware of this conflict between body and mind suggests, speaking about the body states: "Live it as one who will have to move himself from it. Keep in mind that this cohabitation will come to an end: you will be stronger in front of the need to go". [130]

Another aspect treated by Seneca is that of "adjustment". In fact, in modern terms we can state that Seneca's "adjustment" clinically correspond to the stage of overcoming the initial shock. In fact, although in any moment any man and woman can fall "unexpectedly in a difficult situation"[131], Seneca adds, "The greatest worth of nature consists of having given us adaptation. [...] Nobody could withstand a pain that always maintain the same initial intensity".[132] Indeed, also a situation that seems initially unsustainable (Seneca calls it "narrow spaces" in *The Serenity*) can become sustainable through a process of adjustment, of elaboration, and of search of proper strategies: "Also a narrow place, when is well arranged, can become comfortable".[133]

With an actual vision, the philosopher is convinced of the possibility of growth that is gotten in a crisis, that is, that experiential development necessary for a man or woman to progress in his/her life. Nevertheless, it is possible to identify some people "never grown", also adults, whose principal problem consists in the incapability to face crises in their life. Mainly they have never been exposed to, or voluntarily kept back from negative situations and experiences in their existence. This could develop from protective parents, or it is a simple consequence of a fear about nothingness and death. This prevents many from facing the adversities in their life. Seneca quotes a motto of Demetrious the cynical: "No human being is more miserable than the man that has never suffered adversities".[134] This, however, does not have to deny the psychological and spiritual importance of "existential optimism" in people. Yet, at times, such "optimism" can be converted in a sort of "boundless beatitude" where a man and a woman do not accept the adversities of life anymore.

6

Questionnaires on spirituality

✦

6.1. ASSESSING THE NEED FOR SPIRITUAL COUNSELING IN CLIENTS

(Carlo Lazzari, *Spiritual Counseling in Medicine*, iUniverse, 2008)

QUESTIONNAIRE

This questionnaire is about your spiritual life and beliefs. There are no right or wrong answers. However, your opinion will help doctors, nurses, and other people that are helping you to make their best in their medical and emotional assistance. There are no time limitations for completing the questionnaire. However, we suggest that you answer as you usually feel. In addition, this questionnaire is anonymous and the data gathered will be used only by the personnel directly involved in your care. We thank you for your kind cooperation.

◆   ◆   ◆

1. **Spirituality is the strength that I use during adverse life events. It's my personal strategy and it cannot be shared with outsiders.**
    ☐ True, or usually true
    ☐ False, or usually false
    ☐ I can't say

2. **Spirituality means feeling helpful to others in a spirit of brotherhood, and this is the way I cope with adverse life events.**

    ☐ True, or usually true

    ☐ False, or usually false

    ☐ I can't say

3. **Spirituality is being in touch with nature and universe and nobody should interfere.**

    ☐True, or usually true

    ☐ False, or usually false

    ☐ I can't say

4. **Spirituality is the essence of life, something you cannot do without.**

    ☐ True, or usually true

    ☐ False, or usually false

    ☐ I can't say

5. **Spirituality in hospital is a personal walk where nobody should interfere.**

    ☐   True, or usually true

    ☐ False, or usually false

    ☐ I can't say

6. **I am a spiritual person already, and I do not feel I need spiritual counseling.**

    ☐ True, or usually true

    ☐ False, or usually false

    ☐ I can't say

7. **I am not sure that a spiritual counselor can do a lot during my actual condition.**

    ☐ True, or usually true

☐ False, or usually false

☐ I can't say

8. **I do not feel to share my inner spirituality with other people and counselors.**

☐ True, or usually true

☐ False, or usually false

☐ I can't say

9. **I am not spiritual and I do not like to be bothered about.**

☐ True, or usually true

☐ False, or usually false

☐ I can't say

10. **I do not think that talking about spirituality can be of any help during my actual condition.**

☐ True, or usually true

☐ False, or usually false

☐I can't say

11. **I feel a lot of pain and I don't have strength and intention to talk about spiritual things.**

☐ True, or usually true

☐ False, or usually false

☐ I can't say

12. **I am already spiritually oriented and I do not need further guidance in this direction.**

☐ True, or usually true

☐ False, or usually false

☐I can't say

13. **I am already a religious person and I don't feel I need spiritual counseling to cope with events.**

☐ True, or usually true

☐ False, or usually false

☐ I can't say

14. **I have my personal clergyman and s/he is the only person I like to meet for spiritual matters.**

☐ True, or usually true

☐ False, or usually false

☐ I can't say

15. **I believe that spirituality shall not be treated inside hospital or other places apart from a church, chapel, or other religious places.**

☐ True, or usually true

☐ False, or usually false

☐ I can't say

16. **I do not believe that a spiritual counselor has enough knowledge about my religious background.**

☐ True, or usually true

☐   False, or usually false

☐ I can't say

17. **I don't believe that a spiritual counselor can treat topics that are related to my religion.**

☐ True, or usually true

☐ False, or usually false

☐ I can't say

18. **I am afraid that a spiritual counselor might try to influence my religious beliefs.**

☐ True, or usually true

☐ False, or usually false

☐ I can't say

6.2. SPIRITUALITY IS...

(Carlo Lazzari, *Spiritual Counseling in Medicine*, iUniverse, 2008)

QUESTIONNAIRE

This questionnaire carries open-ended questions. In reality these are incomplete assertions. What we ask is to fill them according to your opinion, ideas, feelings, and attitudes. There are no right or false answers. The best way is to write soon without passing too much time in guessing the right answers. There are none. In addition, this questionnaire is anonymous and the data gathered will be used only form the personnel directly involved in your care. We thank you for your kind cooperation.

***

- Spirituality is _____
- Being spiritual for me means _____
- The way I intend to manage spirituality is_____
- What I intend for spirituality is_____
- The best way to deal with adverse life events is_____
- The best way to psychologically deal with diseases is _____
- I feel that spiritual counselors are _____
- I believe that spiritual counselors should _____
- When I feel spiritual, I also feel_____
- I think that the differences between religion and spirituality are____

    _____

- The instruments I use to feel or to be spiritual are _____
- What I would like most to discuss with a spiritual counselor is____

    _____

- What I don't like to discuss with a spiritual counselor is _____

    _____

- What I like less in spirituality is _____
- If I were a spiritual counselor I would_____

6.3. ASSESSING SPIRITUALITY IN HEALTH OPERATORS

(Carlo Lazzari, *Spiritual Counseling in Medicine*, iUniverse, 2008)

QUESTIONNAIRE

This questionnaire is used to assess your involvement in spirituality as an adjunctive instrument in your profession. If you know a little about it, perhaps this questionnaire is not a viable way to assess it. However, after reading the book "Spiritual Counseling in Medicine" you might have gained a different opinion about the use of spirituality in dealing with clients and patients. There are no time limitations for completing the questionnaire. However, we suggest that you answer as you usually feel. Your answers will help your supervisors or other agencies to create better services to clients and to produce educational programs to introduce spirituality as an adjunctive therapeutic force in patients' health and well-being.

***

1. **I feel that spirituality shall be treated by specialized counselors and not by doctors and nurses**

    ☐ True, or usually true

    ☐ False, or usually false

    ☐ I can't say

2. **I have no time to deal with spirituality when dealing with patients.**

    ☐ True, or usually true

    ☐ False, or usually false

    ☐ I can't say

3. **I do not see any interaction between physical-medical therapy and patients' spirituality.**

    ☐ True, or usually true

    ☐ False, or usually false

    ☐ I can't say

4. **I would like to know more about spirituality and spiritual counseling.**

    ☐ True, or usually true

    ☐ False, or usually false

    ☐ I can't say

5. **I use a spiritual approach with my patients.**

☐ True, or usually true

☐ False, or usually false

☐ I can't say

6. **I feel that a spiritual training could be an advantage for my profession.**

    ☐ True, or usually true

    ☐ False, or usually false

    ☐ I can't say

7. **I would like to have more time to interact with my patients in a spiritual way.**

    ☐ True, or usually true

    ☐ False, or usually false

    ☐ I can't say

8. **I feel that the hospital or the place where I work are not the right places where to discuss about spirituality with patients**

    ☐ True, or usually true

    ☐ False, or usually false

    ☐ I can't say

9. **I am a spiritual person**

    ☐ True, or usually true

    ☐False, or usually false

    ☐ I can't say

10. **I use spirituality to deal with difficult cases in my profession.**

    ☐ True, or usually true

    ☐ False, or usually false

    ☐ I can't say

11. **I use spirituality to cope with stress in my profession.**

    ☐True, or usually true

    ☐ False, or usually false

    ☐ I can't say

12. **Spirituality has helped me to deal with suffering people or my patients.**

    ☐ True, or usually true

☐ False, or usually false

☐ I can't say

13. I am afraid to create unwanted reactions in my clients if I started to talk about spiritual things

☐ True, or usually true

☐ False, or usually false

☐ I can't say

14. I don't feel to be the right person to use spiritual counseling.

☐ True, or usually true

☐ False, or usually false

☐ I can't say

15. I feel that spiritual counseling is a waste of time.

☐ True, or usually true

☐ False, or usually false

☐ I can't say

16. I don't like to talk about these things.

☐ True, or usually true

☐ False, or usually false

☐ I can't say

6.4. ASSESSING DOCTORS AND PATIENTS

More than in any other relationships with patients, in spiritual counseling, health professionals need to be sure that "They have seen the patient and that the patient has been seen by them!". This actually means that it is not enough that a doctor, a nurse, a psychologist states that s/he has been empathic and has listened to client's sufferings. Also the client, that has been involved in counseling, shall have the same impression, and shall confirm that the s/he really felt the counselor empathic and communicative. Without this reciprocal check-up of strategies, intentions and skills, spiritual counseling is deprived of its inherent force and meaning: sharing and reciprocity in feelings and ideas. Therefore, the following questionnaire, stands as a verification instrument for counselors and clients when the sections of spiritual therapy begins. The same questionnaire can be repeated several times in order to give to counselors the real status quo of their interventions. The questionnaire is based on a series of core strategies (sharing, being involved, communication, etc.) that make the bricks for the construction of a whole intervention. The questionnaire has been designed on general strategies (listening, talking, etc.) as it works as learning assessment for general strategies in spiritual counseling. It also assesses what has been named 'co-humanity' by Confucius (already met in the book).

QUESTIONNAIRE

Copyright © 2008
iUniverse

(Carlo Lazzari, *Spiritual Counseling in Medicine*, iUniverse, 2008)

Core strategies	Questionnaire for doctors	Questionnaire for clients
Sharing	I feel I have been able to share my feelings in the interaction with my client ☐ True, or usually true ☐ False, or usually false	I feel that my conselor has been able to share with me his feelings ☐ True, or usually true ☐ False, or usually false
Listening	I feel I have been able to listen to client's exposition of the own feelings ☐ True, or usually true ☐ False, or usually false	I feel that my counselor has been attentive when I have exposed my own feelings ☐ True, or usually true ☐ False, or usually false
Communicating	I believe I have communicated in a respectful manner with my client. ☐ True, or usually true ☐ False, or usually false	I feel that my counselor has been respectful when communicating with me ☐ True, or usually true ☐ False, or usually false

Interacting	I suppose I have interacted with my client in order to make him/her feel emotionally supported. ☐ True, or usually true ☐ False, or usually false	I felt emotionally supported when I interacted with my counselor ☐ True, or usually true ☐ False, or usually false
Applying	I feel I have been able to discuss spirituality with my client ☐ True, or usually true ☐ False, or usually false	I feel I have been able to discuss about spirituality with my counselor ☐ True, or usually true ☐ False, or usually false
Moving forward	I believe I've been able to make some progress in promoting my client's feelings of well-being ☐ True, or usually true ☐ False, or usually false	I feel I made some progress in my feelings of well-being ☐ True, or usually true ☐ False, or usually false
Focusing	I suppose I have been focused on the specific issues that were central in client's worries ☐ True, or usually true ☐ False, or usually false	I believe that my counselor has been focused on the issues that were more central for my worries ☐ True, or usually true ☐ False, or usually false
Advocating	I presume I have been able to act for client's when s/he was unable to take care for him/herself: e.g., making a phone call, talking to family doctor or relatives, etc. ☐ True, or usually true ☐ False, or usually false	My counselor has been able to act on my behalf when I was unable to take care of myself: e.g., making a phone call, talking to my family doctor or relatives ☐ True, or usually true ☐ False, or usually false

Sounding	I deem I have treated specific and spiritual issues with my client and s/he felt free to talk me about them ☐ True, or usually true ☐ False, or usually false	I felt free to talk about spirituality with my counselor and I have found him/her receptive on this issue ☐ True, or usually true ☐ False, or usually false

7
Notes

(Endnotes)

1   Lazzari C., "Philosophy and Anthropology of Going", *Thauma*, Edizioni OCD, Roma Morena, N. 1, 2007.

2   Honorè de Balzac, *Teoria del camminare*, [*The theory of walking*], Sugarco Edizioni, 1993; p. 72.

3   Teresa of Ávila (Saint), *L'Anima o il castello del re*, [*The soul or the castle of the king*], San Paolo, Cinisello Balsamo, 2000; p. 37

4   Renoux C., *La preghiera per la pace attribuita a San Francesco*, [*Saint Francis and the Prayer for Peace*], Edizioni Messaggero Padova, 2003; p. 166.

5   Fizzotti E., Scarpelli A., "*Viktor E. Frankl*", Elledici, Turin, 2005; p. 29.

6   Fizzotti E., Scarpelli A., (2005); p. 30.

7   Chakravarthi Ram-Prasad, *Eastern Philosophy*, Weidenfeld & Nicolson, London, 2005; p.77.

8   Belkin S., *In His Image: the Jewish Philosophy of Man As Expressed in Rabbinic Tradition*, Abelard-Schuman Ltd, 1960, USA.

9   De Coppens P. R., *Medicina e Spiritualità*, [*Medicine and Spirituality*], Elvetica Edizioni, Lugano, 2006; p. 163.

10   Duccio Demetrio, *Filosofia del camminare*, [*The philosophy of walking*], Raffaello Cortina Editore, Milano, 2005; p. 9.

11   Honorè de Balzac, (1993); p.53.

12   Garrett M.T., "Hear the Eagle Cry: Native American Spiritual Traditions and Counseling", in Oliver J. Morgan (Ed.), *Counseling and Spirituality*, Lashaska Press, New York, 2007. pp. 141-142.

13 Honorè de Balzac, (1993); p. 60.

14 Duccio Demetrio, (2005); p. 77.

15 Stanard R. P., "Remembering the Lessons of the Angel", in Oliver J. Morgan (Ed.), *Counseling and Spirituality*, Lashaska Press, New York, 2007; p. 129.

16 Garrett, (2007); p. 147.

17 Josemaria Escrivà de Balaguer, *Cammino*, [*Walk*], Oscar Mondadori, Milan, 1991; p. 115.

18 Duccio Demetrio, (2005); p. 48.

19 Morel C., *Dizionario dei simboli, dei miti e delle credenze*, [*Dictionary of symbols, myths, and beliefs*], Giunti, Florence, Italy, 2006; p. 806-807.

20 Morel C., (2006); p. 201.

21 Honorè de Balzac, (1993); p.52.

22 Morel C., (2006); p. 200.

23 The ring, in Latin *anellus*, which means "unity and totality", also represents an agreement between man and the Lord, which is also expressed by the Shepherd Ring, this being the ring of the Pope". Morel C., (200); pp. 54-55.

24 Jacobson, Jr., C. Jeff, Luckhaupt, Sara E. DeLaney, Sheli, Tsevat, Joel. "Religio-biography, coping, and meaning-making among persons with HIV/AIDS". *Journal for the Scientific Study of Religion*. 45(1) 2006 March; pp. 39-56.

25 Jacobson, et al. (2006); pp. 39-56.

26 Authors, "In the dark: hidden abuses against detained youths in Rio de Janeiro", *Human Rights Watch,* Vol. 17, N. 2(B).

27 Honorè de Balzac, (1993); p. 56.

28 Honorè de Balzac, (1993); p. 53.

29 Samuel Z. Klausner, "The social psychology of courage", *Review of Religious Research*, Vol. 3, No. 2. (Autumn, 1961), pp. 63-72.

30 Samuel Z. Klausner, (1961); p. 68.

31 Samuel Z. Klausner, (1961); p. 69.

32 Duccio Demetrio, (2005); p. 277.

33 Ventura B. M., "L'insegnamento della filosofia e l'universo giovanile" ["Teaching of phylosophy and the youth universe"], speech given to the Training Corse for teachers of philosophy, "Didactics of Phylosophy and Brocca programs", cured by the IRRSAE-Marche (Italy), during November 13th 1966 at Civitanova Marche (Italy).

34 Morel C., (2006); p. 201.

35 Honorè de Balzac, (1993); p.78.

36 Honorè de Balzac, (1993); p. 70.

37 Frankl V. E., *Senso e valori per l'esistenza*, [*Meanings and values for life*] Città Nuova Editrice, Roma, II ed., 1998; p. 42.

38 White John, (*The Meaning of Science and Spirit*), *L'Incontro di Scienza e Spirito*, (Italian Translation) Pratiche Editrice, Il Saggiatore, Milan, 2001; p. 263.

39 Mental Health Foundation, *The Impact of Spirituality on Mental Health*, Copyright, 2006. www.mentalhealth.org.uk

40 Royal College of Psychiatrists, Spirituality and Psychiatry Special Interest Group, *Spirituality and Mental Health*, June 200:http://www.rcpsych.ac.uk/college/specialinterestgroups/spirituality.aspx.

41 Mental Health Foundation, (2006).

42 Nathan, M., "The Healing Power of Love", Report of the meeting on 8th November 2001 at the Royal College of Psychiatrists.

43 Thompson Mel, *Philosophy of Religion*, Hodder Headline, London, 1997; p. 1.

44 Lazzari C., Masino M. A., *L'amore che cura: guida alla relazione d'aiuto*, [*The Healing Love: a guide to the helping relationship*] FrancoAngeli, Milan, 2007b.

45 Herranz Ponzalo, "The words of José Maria Escrivà de Balaguer to physicians, nurses and patients", Chaplainship of the Biolmedical University Campus in Rome, 1976.

46 Koenig H. G., *Spirituality in Patient Care: Why, How, When, and What*, Templeton Foundation Press, Philadelphia & London, 2002; p. 2.

47 Chakravarthi Ram-Prasad, cited; p. 79.

48 Shapiro, A. K.; Shapiro, E. "The Placebo: Is It Much Ado about Nothing", In *The Placebo Effect: An Interdisciplinary Exploration*; Harrington, A., E.; Harvard University Press; Cambridge, MA, 1997; pp. 12-36.

49 Hróbjartsson, A. "The uncontrollable placebo effect", *European J. Clin. Pharmacol*, 1996, No 50, pp. 345-348.

50 Koenig H. G., (2002); p. 49.

51 Spiro, H, *The Power of Hope: A Doctor's Perspective*. Yale University Press, New Haven, CT, 1998; p. 278.

52 Hart Carol, "The Mysterious Placebo Effect", *Modern Drug Discovery*, July/August, 1999, 2(4), pp. 30-40.

53 Lasagna, L. "The Placebo Effect", *J. Allergy Clin. Immunol*, 1986, No. 78, pp. 161-165.

54 Shapiro & Shapiro, (1997).

55 Swartzman, L. C.; Burkell, J., "Expectations and the placebo effect in clinical drug trials", *Clin. Pharmacol. Ther.*, 1998; No. 64; pp. 1-7.

56 Hart Carol, (1999).

57   Morel C., (2006).

58   Pontiggia (ed.), *Vassily Kandinsky. The Spiritual in the Art*, Bompiani Publ., Milan, 1993; pp. 18-19.

59   Lamparelli C. (ed.), *Montaigne: Physical and Spiritual Wellbeing*, Mondadori Publ., Milan, 2006; pp. 48-49.

60   Lazzari C., "L'ospedale come rete di relazioni da persona a persona" [The Hospital as a Network of relationships amongst people], *MEDIC*, Vol. 15, N. 2, August 2007, pp. 82-87.

61   *Catechismo della chiesa cattolica* [*Catechism of the Catholic Church*], San Paolo e Libreria Editrice Vaticana [Saint Paul and Vatican Bookstore Publisher], 2005.

62   Baetz Marilyn, Griffin Ron, Bown Rudy, Marcoux Gene, "Spirituality and Psychiatry in Canada: Psichiatric Practice Compared With Patient Expectations", *Can. J. Psychiatry*, Vol. 49, No. 4, April 2004.

63   Baetz et al., (2004); p. 270.

64   Kammann R., Campbell K., "Illusory correlation in popular beliefs about the causes of Happiness", *New Zealand Psychologists*, 1982 (Nov), Vol 11 (2); pp. 52-63.

65   Rimland B, "The Altruism Paradox", *Psychologivcal Reports*, 1982 (Oct.), Vol.51 (2); pp 521-522.

66   Dimberg, U., "Facial Reactions to Facial Expressions", *Psychophysiology*, 1982 (Nov.), Vol. 19(6); pp. 643-647.

67   Davidson R., Fox N., "Asymmetrical Brain Activity Discriminated Between Positive and Negative Affective Stimuli in Human Infants", *Science*, 1982 (Dec), Vol. 218 (4578); pp: 1235-1237.

68   Tatarkiewicz W., *Analysis of Happiness*, Warsawa: Martinus Nijhoff/ The Hague PWN, Polish Scientific Publishers, 1976.

69   Thorndike, in Tatarkiewicz W., (1976).

70   Tatarkiewicz W., (1976).

71   Brinton D., *The Pursuit of Happiness*, Philadelphia, David McKay Publisher, 1984.

72   McGill V. J., *The Idea of Happiness*, New York, Praeger, 1967.

73   Harry J, "Evolving Sources of Happiness for Men Over the Life Cycle: A Structural Analysis", *Journal of Marriage & The Family*, 1967 (May), Vol. 38 (2); pp. 289-296.

74   McGill V. J, (1967).

75   Rahner K., *Happiness Through Prayer*, Westminster, Maryland, Newman Press, 1965.

76   Russel B., *The Conquest of Happiness*, New York, Horace Liveright, 1930.

77   Russel B., (1930).

78   Taylor R., "Yes Words Can Hurt", *The Plain Truth*, July/August 1984, Vol. 49 (7); pp. 24-25.

79   Weidman Gibbs Harriett, Achterberg-Lawlis Jeanne, "Spiritual values and death anxiety: implications for counseling with terminal cancer patients", *Journal of Counseling Psychology*, 1978, Vol. 26, N. 6, 563-569

80   Sadock B. J., Sadock V.A., *Kaplan & Sadock's Pocket Handbook di Psichiatria Clinica* [*Kaplan & Sadock's Pocket Handbook of Clinical Psychiatry*], Centro Scientifico Editore [Italian translation], 2003; p. 154.

81   Miner-Williams Denise, "Putting a puzzle together: making spirituality meaningful for nursing using an evolving theoretical framework", *Journal of Clinical Nursing*, Blackwell Publishing Ltd, 2006, 15, 811-821; p. 813.

82   Miner-Williams, (2006); p. 815-816.

83   Miner-Williams, (2006); p. 816.

84   Morgan J. O, "Counseling's Fifth Force", in *Counseling and Spirituality*, Lahaska Press, Houghton Mifflin Company, Boston, New York, 2007; p. 2.

85   Budd, C. F., "An Air Force Model of Psychologist-Chaplain Collaboration", *Professional Psychology: Research and Practice*, 1999, Vol. 30, 552-556; pp. 555-556.

86   Tolstoj, L. N., *La Morte di Ivan Il'ic* [*The Death of Ivan Il'ic*], La Spiga, Milan, 1995.

87   Tolstoj, L. N., (1995); p. 41.

88   Tolstoj, L. N., (1995); p. 41.

89   Tolstoj, L. N., (1995); p. 42.

90   Tolstoj, L. N., (1995); p. 39.

91   Tolstoj, L. N, (1995); p. 54.

92   Tolstoj, L. N., (1995); p. 54-55.

93   Tolstoj, L. N., (1995); p. 81.

94   Tolstoj, L. N., (1995); p. 84.

95   Lazzari C., *Vivere Serenamente* [*A way of living peacefully: how to psychologically face serious illnesses and existential crises*], Bologna, Pitagora Editrice, 1996.

96   Hugo Victor, *L'ultimo giorno di un condannato a morte* [*The Last Day of a Death Row Inmate*], Rome, Newton Compton, 1993; p. 41.

97   Hugo Victor, (1993); p. 41.

98   Brooks C., "Where Our Spirits Touch: The Process of Counseling and Spirituality", in Morgan O. J. (Ed.), *Counseling and Spirituality*, Lahaska Press, New York, 2007; p.51.

99   Hugo Victor, (1993); p. 45.
100   Hugo Victor, (1993); p. 45.
101   Hugo Victor, (1993); p. 48.
102   Hugo Victor, (1993); p. 59.
103   Hugo Victor, (1993); p. 80.
104   Camus A., *La Peste*, [*The Plague*], Bompiani, Milan, 4th Edition, 1993; p. 47.
105   Camus, (1993); p. 56.
106   Camus, (1993); p. 58.
107   Klausner Samuel Z., "Social Psychology of Courage", *Review of Religious Research*, Vol. 3, No. 2. Autumn, 1961; pp. 63-72.
108   Klausner Samuel Z., (1961).
109   Klausner Samuel Z., (1961).
110   Lazzari C., *Guida alla comunicazione con la persona in crisi e con il malato grave*, [*A guide to the communication with the sick person, and with the severely ill patient*], Pitagora Editrice, Bologna, 1995; pp. 1-8.
111   Baetz Marilyn, Griffin Ron, Bown Rudy, Marcoux Gene, "Spirituality and Psychiatry in Canada: Psychiatric Practice Compared With Patient Expectations", *Can. J. Psychiatry*, Vol. 49, No. 4, April 2004.
112   Cervantes J. M., Parham, T., "Toward a Meaningful Spirituality for People of Color: Lessons for the Counseling Practitioner", *Cultural Diversity and Ethnic Minority Psychology*, Vol. 11, No. 1, 69-81; p. 76.
113   Koenig H.G., 2002; p. 24.
114   Frankl V., *Dio nell'inconscio: psicoterapia e religione* [*God in the unconscious: Psychotherapy and Religion*], Morcelliana, Brescia, 2000; p. 84. [Original title: Der unbewuâteGott. Psychotherapie und Religion, © Kösel Verlag – München 1973].
115   Culliford L., "Spiritual care and psychiatric treatment: an introduction", *Advances in Psychiatric Treatment*, 2002, Vol. 8, pp. 249-261; p. 255.
116   McCullough M. E., "Research on Religion-Accomodative Counseling: Review and Meta-Analysis", *Journal of Counseling Psychology*, Vol. 46, No. 1, 92-98; p. 96.
117   Rose M. E., Westefeld J. S., Ansley T. N., "Spiritual Issues in Counseling: Client's Beliefs and Preferences", *Journal of Counseling Psychology*, 2001, Vol. 48, No. 1, 67-71; p.62.
118   Rose M. E., Westefeld J. S., Ansley T. N., (2001); p. 62.
119   Rose M. E., Westefeld J. S., Ansley T. N., (2001); p. 62.
120   Lucio Anneo Seneca, *La Brevità Della Vita* [*The Brevity Of Life*], La Spiga publisher, Milan, 1993.
121   Lucio Anneo Seneca, (1993); p. 11.
122   Lucio Anneo Seneca, (1993); p. 11.

123   Lucio Anneo Seneca, (1993); p. 12.
124   Lucio Anneo Seneca, (1993); p. 14.
125   Lucio Anneo Seneca, (1993); p. 14.
126   Marchesi C (ed.), *Seneca: la Dottrina Morale* [*Seneca: The Moral Doctrine*], Laterza, Bari, 1994, pp-68-71.
127   Marchesi C (ed.), (1994); p. 40.
128   Marchesi C (ed.), (1994); p. 40.
129   Reale G.T. (ed.), *Seneca: Breviario* [*Seneca: Breviary*], Rusconi, Milan 1994; p. 31.
130   Reale G.T., (1994); p. 46.
131   Scaffidi Abate M., (Ed.), *Seneca: L'Ozio e La Serenità* [*Seneca: Idleness and Serenity*], Newton Compton, Rome, 1994, p. 71.
132   Scaffidi Abate M., (1994); p. 73.
133   Scaffidi Abate M., (1994); p. 73.
134   Scaffidi Abate M., (1994); p. 76.